Sound, in Any of its Forms,
is a Source of Energy.

As a source of energy, it can be used to interact with other energies. Sound—whether through music, voice, or other sources—is effective as a tool to alter the electro-magnetic fields and impulses of an individual or an environment.

This means that if an imbalance has occurred within the body's normal electro-magnetic parameters (whether it is a dysfunction of a specific organ or of a particular system) we can utilize sacred sound in one of its forms or combinations to help restore homeostasis, alleviate pain or to accelerate healing.

As an energy source, it can also be a tool for the change of consciousness. It facilitates concentration, relaxation, learning, creativity and an increased awareness of psycho-spiritual states. It can interact with and help alter brain wave patterns to facilitate this process.

About the Author

Ted Andrews is a full-time author, student and teacher in the metaphysical and spiritual fields. He conducts seminars, symposiums, and workshops and lectures throughout the country on many facets of ancient mysticism. Ted works with past-life analysis, auric interpretation, numerology, the Tarot and the Qabala as methods of developing and enhancing inner potential. He is a clairvoyant and certified in spiritual mediumship, basic hypnosis, and acupressure. Ted is also involved in the study and use of herbs as an alternative path. In addition to writing several books, he is a contributing author to various metaphysical magazines.

To Write to the Author

If you wish to contact the author or would like more information about this book, please write to the author in care of Llewellyn Worldwide, and we will forward your request. Both the author and publisher appreciate hearing from you and learning of your enjoyment of this book and how it has helped you. Llewellyn Worldwide cannot guarantee that every letter written to the author can be answered, but all will be forwarded. Please write to:

Ted Andrews
c/o Llewellyn Worldwide
2143 Wooddale Drive, Dept. 978-0-87542-018-9
Woodbury, MN 55125-2989, U.S.A.

Please enclose a self-addressed, stamped envelope for reply,
or $1.00 to cover costs. If outside the U.S.A., enclose international
postal reply coupon.

SACRED SOUNDS

MAGIC & HEALING
THROUGH WORDS & MUSIC

TED ANDREWS

Llewellyn Publications
Woodbury, Minnesota

FIRST EDITION
Thirteenth Printing, 2008

Cover design by Kevin R. Brown
Images © Photodisc

Library of Congress Cataloging-in-Publication Data
Andrews, Ted, 1952–
   Sacred sounds: transformation through music and word /
     by Ted Andrews.—1st ed.
      p.   cm. — (Llewellyn practical guides to
          personal power)
   Includes bibliographical references.
   ISBN 13: 978-0-87542-018-9
   ISBN 10: 0-87542-018-4
   1. Magic. 2. Sound—Miscellanea. 3. Music and magic.
4. Speech—Miscellanea. I. Title. II. Series.
BF1623.S57A53   1992
133.4'3—dc20   92-45962
                                               CIP

Llewellyn Worldwide does not participate in, endorse, or have any authority or responsibility concerning private business transactions between our authors and the public.

    All mail addressed to the author is forwarded but the publisher cannot, unless specifically instructed by the author, give out an address or phone number.

Llewellyn Publications
A Division of Llewellyn Worldwide, Ltd.
2143 Wooddale Drive, Dept. 978-0-87542-018-9
Woodbury, MN 55125-2989
www.llewellyn.com
Llewellyn is a registered trademark of Llewellyn Worldwide, Ltd.
Printed in the United States of America

Other Books by Ted Andrews

Animal Speak
Dream Alchemy
Enchantment of the Faerie Realm
The Healer's Manual
How to Heal with Color
How to Meet & Work with Spirit Guides
How to See & Read the Aura
How to Uncover Your Past Lives
How to Do Psychic Readings Through Touch
Imagick
The Magical Name
Magickal Dance
The Occult Christ
The Sacred Power in Your Name
Simplified Qabala Magic

To everyone who ever heard a story that thrilled them, a song that stirred them, or an idea that changed them.

SACRED SOUNDS

Acknowledgements

I would like to thank those who have added to my appreciation and love for music. These include my parents, and also my teachers: particularly my first piano instructor, Mrs. Allison, who showed me how to have fun with the piano and my grade school music teacher, Susan Gilbert, who demonstrated the power of weaving music and story together. I also wish to thank Virgina Blakelock and her parents. Whout the inspiriation of Virginia's playing and the loving spiritual gift of the piano from her parents, a beautiful part of my life might never have come to be. My gratitude, my thoughts and my prayers are with them always.

TABLE OF CONTENTS

The Heart of the Lost Traditions

Every society expresses its truths in the manner most acceptable and most easily understood by its members. When explored, the truths of one society are not as different from the others as we often believe. There are common threads and methods which run through them all. At the heart of all the lost traditions was the teaching of the power of the WORD—the ability to use sound, voice, and music to create changes in oneself or in others.

Every society, tradition, and religion has had teachings both magical and wondrous. The relaying and demonstrating of these wondrous teachings fell to individuals who were schooled in the natural and spiritual laws of the universe. These priests/priestesses/magicians—regardless of how they were labeled in their society—used the secret arts of sound, music, and words to teach, heal, and enlighten. They imbued their words with the power of imagination and the power of music. The myths, the stories, the poems and songs were used to bridge the different worlds of life and the different modes of consciousness. They can be used to do so again.

This tradition of the Word is not truly lost. It is obscure, but it still lives within the tales, the myths, and the songs of the past. Remnants exist and can be gathered and re-expressed with new life today. The heart of the lost tradition of the Word still lives within the imagination of all.

"Let there be Light" is the divine prompting to awaken and use the creative imagination. The Elizabethan writers used the phrase "intending the mind." This "intending" is the fixing of the mind upon something, focusing with a clear and steady flame, a flame that brings illumination. We must intend the mind to create new expressions of this lost tradition. We must fill our words, myths, and music with the power of the imagination.

All words and sounds are essentially magical, and yet the paradox is that they must also be rendered magical. The words and sounds are seeds, holding the essence of magic and light. Unless those seeds are nurtured and helped to take root, the magic either lies dormant or it grows within our life in peculiar ways.

The lost tradition of the Word is a living, creative art. It involves understanding and using the power of sound, music, and words. It involves the art of magical storytelling to help ourselves and others leap from the endless cycles and spirals of day to day life and find a direct and quicker passage to achievement. It involves opening to heal and be healed through music and sound. It involves opening to seership through the sheer force of poetry and song. It involves opening the magical visions and dreams of life.

The tradition of the Word is the fairy chest of treasures. The treasures within can be used by each of us in our own way. The treasures can be exchanged for something wanted or needed, or they may be enjoyed for themselves. This chest, this tradition, comes with great responsibility. It demands concentration. It demands that we learn to use—not waste—the treasures. It demands understanding the profound influence sound has, and how it affects all of us.

You must remember that a tradition is not a religion. It is a tool by which you can unfold the creative potential that lies within. It is a tool to create circumstances in your normal day-to-day life that can open the doors to your potential.

The lost tradition of the Word is the riddle of paradox. Once learned, there must be a joy in its sharing. It is something that you keep, even while you give it away. You must never hoard it and never give it directly, or its virtue will be lost. You must use it to stay upon the higher path and yet use it also to know when to step off. You can work with it to have a way of your own and to have it entirely. You can take the old and express it anew.

> There is a kind of death to every story when it leaves the speaker and becomes impaled for all time on clay tablets or the written and printed page. To take it from the page, to create it again into living substance, this is the challenge . . .
>
> —Ruth Sawyer,
> *The Way of the Storyteller*

PART ONE

The Secret Power of the Word

In the spheres a wonderful harmony of sound is being produced eternally, and from that source have ALL things been created.
—Florence Crane

CHAPTER ONE

The Science of Sacred Sound

Sacred sound—whether as prayer, music, song, incantation or chants—is a vital force which permeates every aspect of creation. In the New Testament, the Book of John states: "In the beginning was the Word and the Word was with God and the Word was God . . ." (John 1:1). In the Ethiopian cosmology, God is said to have created both Himself and the universe through the utterance of his own name. In Egypt, Thoth used words to create the universe, calling out over the waters "Come unto me . . ." Even in the early Babylonian cosmology, the gods mothered by Tiamut in the waters of life did not emerge as beings until they were named.

Sound has always been considered a direct link between humanity and the divine. At some point, all of the ancient mystery schools taught their students the use of sound as a creative and healing force. It is considered the oldest form of healing, and it was a predominant part of the early teachings of the Greeks, Chinese, East Indians, Tibetans, Egyptians, American Indians, Mayas, and the Aztecs.

The Chinese healers used "singing stones"—thin flat pieces of jade which would emit various musical tones when struck. One of these tones was designated the "kung" or great tone of Nature. It corresponds in our own musical scale to the tone of F or F-sharp. The Sufis consider "Hu" to be the ultimate creative sound. The Tibetans considered the tones of F-sharp, A and G to be the three powerful and sacred tones of the world. "Om," "Aum" and "Amen" were believed by many ancient societies and traditions to represent all the sounds the human voice was capable of expressing and manifesting in the physical world. The Essenes, a third sect of Jews living in the world at the time of the master Christ Jesus, were dynamic healers. Their name comes from a word "asaya" which means to heal or to doctor. They were schooled in the mystic and healing arts of sound and nature.

Much of what we know of the past regarding the teachings of sacred sound comes through the musical and architectural remnants of those times. Sculptures in Baghdad (dating around 4000 B.C.) show several musicians playing harps and flutes. Music and sound as an art form was well-developed by the Egyptians, Hindus, Chinese, and Japanese. By the time Egypt built the pyramids and sphinxes, it had organized choruses of 12,000 voices and orchestras of 600 pieces. Many believe it was through their use of directed and controlled sound that much of the heaviest labor was accomplished on the pyramids.

From the early Greeks come some of the earliest scientific observations on sound and its true nature and effects. The Greek master Orpheus was to many of the ancient mystics the theologian *par excellence*. He was a poet, a musician, theologian and even an interpreter of the gods. He was considered the first of the world's singers. The Greek mythologies speak of him as the son of Apollo, the father of truth, wisdom and divination. His mother was

Calliope, one of the Muses. It was from her that he received his gift of music, music capable of moving immoveable objects.

Orpheus is often considered the great hierophant of the Dionysian Mysteries. He instructed the Greeks in magic and music, and the power of his healing voice and music was ascribed to certain magical formula, incantations and charms that are inscribed in the ancient Orphic Tablets.

The name Orpheus means "he who heals by the light" and it is quite probable that it was a title of a particular level of healing achievement (through the application of sacred sound).

> Initiation into the Orphic Mysteries, performed by priestly sorcerers and healers, was supposed to spare the soul the cycle of reincarnation .... To avoid new birth, certain magical formula were learnt by heart; the dead man was allowed to drink the waters of a living spring, whereupon he cast off his carnal nature in which sin inhered, and thus purified, "reigned among the heroes."
>
> — S. Reinach,
> *Orpheus*

The Pythagorean and Platonic Schools of Wisdom would arise partly from the Orphic mystery teachings. Pythagoras created the modern musical octave in an attempt to reveal the relationship between musical notes and the mathematical principles of the universe.

Other Greeks and Romans would add to our modern awareness of the physical and metaphysical effects of sound. Aristotle presented humanity with one of the earliest theories of how sound was transmitted through the air. Pollio (*circa* 20 B.C.) lent tremendous insight into the acoustics of buildings and the power of echo and reverberation. With reverberation, diffusion of sound occurs. A reverberated sound is one which re-echoes many times. These reverberations impinge upon the ear and the body, giving the impression of being within a sea of sound. It is this effect that was created through strong, repeated invocations and chants, filling the temple or room with the force or energy being invoked. This helped to create a space acceptable for its actual physical manifestation or for the raising of the consciousness of the individual to a sense of unity with the divine force. The Greek amphitheaters exhibited highly advanced knowledge of acoustical properties. They were free from noise. They increased intelligibility of speech, and they retained the richness of the music. The Greeks even constructed shells to further direct and reflect sounds in specific patterns. (This would eventually carry over into the Gothic cathedrals constructed by masons schooled in such techniques. The chants and songs would lift the consciousness of the individual to new heights.)

Many societies had forbidden certain kinds of music, especially in the formative years of the children. There was more extensive awareness of how sound played upon all aspects of humanity and could trigger problems in health and balance. In those societies which practiced "musical restraint," part of the overall education of the individual included training in the musical arts.

By the time of the Roman Empire many of the restraints were no longer practiced, except in the more closed societies and traditions. It is unique that one of the most powerful emperors of Rome, Julius Caesar, recognized the influence of sound upon the well-being of people to the extent that he went so far as to issue a noise ordinance and even had straw laid over the city streets to soften the noise.

Since the time of the early Greeks and the Roman Empire, the teachings of sacred sound and the power of the Word has been passed down through what we now generically call the "bardic tradition." Through the Greek rhapsodists, the English bards, the French troubadours, the African griots, the Norse skalds, the Navajo singers, the power to teach, heal, and raise consciousness through sound, music, and voice has been kept alive. Although today most people are either unaware or simply ignore the significance and preponderance of sound within their lives, this ancient knowledge is even more important within a technological society in which we are constantly bombarded by extraneous sounds.

Sound is a major contributing factor to our present state of consciousness. The difference between the random sounds of daily life and the focused use of sacred sound is that the latter produces harmony rather than dissonance. When we learn to produce and direct sacred sound through our energy centers (chakras) to the physical body, balance occurs which energizes our entire energy system. We then have greater access to our true essence and its manifestation within our day-to-day life circumstances. We have greater health on all levels, and we can disrupt negative qualities and patterns as they arise within our physical and subtle bodies. We transmute them into positive ones. We begin to direct the alchemical processes of life—and it all begins with understanding the principles of sacred sound.

THE SACRED SOUND PRINCIPLE OF RESONANCE

There are basic sound principles that we must understand if we are to apply the secret power of the Word effectively within our lives. They serve as the foundation for all healing, enlightenment and the magic associated with the uses of sound, music and voice. *Resonance* is the most important principle of sound in any form. It designates the ability of a vibration to reach out through vibrational waves to set off a similar vibration in another body.

Physics teaches that life is composed of atoms which contain protons and electrons. These are electrically and magnetically charged particles of energy. They are in constant motion—at times more so than at others, making their movements audible. The sound vibrations that physics speaks of are connected to the vibrations or undulations of atoms and molecules within the air.

The undulations in the air cause pressure changes, resulting in sections of the air becoming denser and others more rarefied. These occur one after another, in the manner of the rippling caused by a stone tossed into a pond. The sound vibrations set the air molecules in motion. They ripple outward, propelled to and impacting upon any receiving set—such as the human body. Audible sound vibrations enter the ear, causing the eardrum to vibrate. These vibrations are picked up by the nerves which translate them into sound. When it is windy, it is more difficult to hear because the wind scatters the molecules, preventing them from condensing.

Condensed vibrations alternate with rarefied vibrations.

The principle of resonance is most easily demonstrated through the use of a tuning fork and a piano. If we were to strike a tuning fork keyed to the tone of middle C and then raise the lid upon the piano, softly feeling along the piano wires, we would find that the piano wire for middle C would be vibrating. The vibrations of the tuning fork triggered a response in that which was of a similar frequency.

Every cell within our body is a sound resonator. It has the capability of responding to any other sound outside of the body. Every organ, in which cells of like vibration have gathered to form that organ, will respond as a group to particular sound vibrations. The various systems in the body will also respond to sound vibrations, as will various emotional, mental and spiritual states of consciousness. The human body is a bio-electrical system. The bio-electrical energy is created in varying frequencies through muscular actions and can be altered, strengthened or balanced through the use of sacred sound. This occurs through the quality of resonance.

We can stimulate an immense number of sympathetic vibrations within our body and mind by learning to direct and control our voice, and by using certain musical instruments, tones and forms of music. Where there is imbalance, we can use directed sound to bring the imbalance back into its normal parameters.

Our body knows how to take care of itself. Unfortunately, we do not always assist it in its process. Through lack of exercise and poor diet, our system can get out of balance. When this occurs, the body must perform twice the work. It must first go about the job of restoring balance before it can correct and eliminate what created the imbalance. We can use sacred sound techniques to restore the balance and thus allow the body to do what it knows best.

In metaphysics we are taught that we are a microcosm of the universe. This means that we have all energies to some degree within us. In our physical or subtle bodies we have all of the inherent energy vibrations of the universe. This vibration can be both physical and non-physical, involving tangible and intangible energies. Most humans find it easiest to perceive the physical nature of a vibration. It is definable and more tangible, such as pulsations in the air from sound or from other sources. Vibrations that are not recognizably physical still affect us and can be sensed and felt if the intuitive and physical perceptions are heightened.

We have a capability of resonating or responding to all sound vibration—positive or negative. We need to be alert to the sounds around us and to strengthen our energies so that only the beneficial sounds can permeate our individual energy fields.

The transmission of a resonant vibration requires three things. First, there must be an original vibrating energy source. This can be thought, sounds, colors, musical instruments, or voices. Almost anything can set in motion the energy between two destinations.

Second, there must be a transmitting medium. With few exceptions, almost anything is a good medium for transmitting sound vibrations. For humans, air is the most common carrier. The motion of the vibrating origin is passed from one molecule of air to another and so on. The human ear can pick up vibrations between 16 and 20,000 vibrations per second. However, the human body will still feel pulsations that are not heard. Those who develop the psychic ability known as clairaudience have raised their own energy to pick up even higher vibrational rates.[1]

Third, there must be a receiver of the vibration, something which will receive and respond to the energy or sound vibration being sent. Remember, our entire body is a sound resonator with a capability of responding to a multitude of vibrations. This reception and response to outside vibrations can occur in a sympathetic manner or through a forced manner.

Sympathetic vibration (or resonance) occurs when two or more bodies have similar or identical vibrational frequencies, making them more easily compatible. There is an innate sympathy. This is sometimes known as free resonance. The important factor in sympathetic resonance is the readiness of the individual to respond to a particular frequency. This reveals much about the relationships we form. In this aspect also lies the answer to the occult axiom: "When the student is ready, the teacher appears."

Through sympathetic resonance, group rapport is established, and individuals respond to the energies of others. Because of this quality of resonance, teaching is simply helping someone realize what they already know. In those groups that come together for a singular purpose, that purpose serves as the media for establishing sympathetic resonance among the group participants.

Forced resonance occurs when two energy systems have different frequencies, and the stronger vibration is transmitted to the other by force. This has both positive and negative aspects to it. (These sound principles are neutral and it is only their application which determines the inherent "goodness" or "evil.") Many forms and manifestations of black magic and the abuse of mind power can come as a result of forced resonance.[2] It is because of its sheer force that many may get caught up in its practice. It is through forced resonance that such phenomena as peer pressure also occurs. The combined force or energy of the group overwhelms the energy of the single individual and forces it into resonance with that group.

If understood and used correctly, forced resonance can be used to overcome imbalanced conditions in the body and to force various organs and systems back within their normal parameters—restoring homeostasis. High pitches can be used to shatter negative, limiting energy patterns. They can be used to create an intensity within the individual's energy field that can lead to enrichment.

These aspects of resonance help explain the sympathy and antipathy we experience with various people within our lives. It is also this quality of sacred sound that allows us in the physical to contact and attune ourselves to those entities and energies in the spiritual or more ethereal dimensions of life.

When two or more energies or vibrating realities come into sync or resonance with one another—whether through sympathy or force—entrainment occurs. The individuals come into phase, blending and mingling into a mixed harmony of vibrations. This is why occult groups are only as strong as the weakest member. Because our cells and our entire physical organism are a complex set of sound oscillators and receptors, we are subject to forced resonance and even entrainment with the outside world. When this occurs through forced resonance, we see participation in cults, black magic, and extreme political, social and religious activities.

When sounds are impinged upon the human body, resonance can take either a beneficial or detrimental effect. The human body is bio-electrical. Our auric fields are electro-magnetic energy fields surrounding the physical body. We are constantly giving off (electrical aspect) and absorbing (magnetic aspect) energy. Every time we interact with another person, there is an exchange of energy vibrations. If we are around many people throughout the day, we may accumulate a tremendous amount of energy debris. Unless we learn to recognize this and cleanse our fields of it, we can end up with physical, emotional, mental and spiritual problems. The techniques outlined throughout the rest of this book will assist you in cleansing, balancing and strengthening your own energy system through directed use of sound, music and voice.

Part of the secret power of the Word involves learning to control and direct our resonance with other energies. We must develop the ability to discriminate among energies. We must learn to use specific techniques to keep our energies vibrant, strong and resonant so that we only respond to that which we desire and direct.

SACRED SOUND PRINCIPLES OF RHYTHM, MELODY AND HARMONY

There are other principles that all of the ancient societies had in common in their teachings of sacred sound. They all taught that rhythm could effect changes in physical states, melody could effect changes in emotional and mental states and harmony was capable of lifting the consciousness to spiritual awareness. Chants, mantras, prayers, songs, stories, music and speech must employ rhythm, melody and harmony to achieve union of body, mind and spirit.

In almost every society there has been what was termed "The Song of the Absolute" or the three-fold song. Three numerologically is the great creative number. It is the number of the artist, the musician, the poet and the mystic. This threefold song employs three aspects of sacred sound principle:

Rhythm—from which comes all motion in the universe.

Melody—from which comes the interaction between the divine in the physical and our own interactions with other life forms.

Harmony—from which comes the true spiritual power manifesting in the universe and in humans as our interaction with all elements of life are harmonized.

Rhythm is the pulse of life and it affects all physical conditions. Rhythm can be used to restore the normal, healthy pulse within a person. Being exposed to a regular, steady rhythm triggers a resonance with the body's own natural rhythms. The rhythms outside of us can trigger a forced resonance and entrainment of our inner rhythms. This has both beneficial and detrimental applications.

Some rhythms are abnormal and can create problems. They can overstimulate the inner pulse. They can force the normal heart rhythm into one that is counter to a healthy pulse within the body. One such rhythm is anapestic. This was a rhythm used by the Rolling Stones in some of their earlier music of the sixties. It is also a rhythm that is employed by some modern punk and heavy metal rock and roll bands. In the sixties, studies were conducted because individuals were experiencing breathing and heart arrhythmias linked to the music.

The normal heartbeat follows a pattern of "Da-da Da-da Da-da." An anapestic rhythm sets up a heart rhythm of "da-da-Da da-da-Da." This is counter to the normal heartbeat rhythm, which can affect all of the internal body functions. This is only one of many rhythms that can counter the normal rhythms of the body. Any rhythm that is strong and to which we are exposed long enough can create a condition of excitation and hyperactivity within the body as it is brought into resonance with it.

Steady, directed rhythms restore the body's rhythms when they are out of balance. For instance, individuals with heart conditions benefit strongly from listening to Baroque music. This form of classical music has a rhythm that is soothing and healing to the pulsations of the heart. It is a form of music being used more commonly now in cardiac surgery. Its rhythms promote healing and strengthening of the heart.

Rhythmic patterns have always been a part of ritual and healing. Pure, specific rhythms were associated with definite ideas, experiences and physiological processes. Drum and knocking patterns exist for the emotions and for exploration of inner consciousness. Many shamanic practices involve using the drumbeat to induce an altered state of consciousness and even a trance condition. The participant concentrates on the drum beat and follows it, as if riding the drumbeat on a mythical journey to an inner state of being. This allows access into levels of consciousness that are normally inaccessible. In shamanism, the drum establishes a kind of bridge enabling the shaman to connect to a magical state of consciousness.

In healing practices, rhythm (whether expressed through drums, rattles, bells or gongs) can energize and stimulate our basic primal energies. Rhythms—especially through percussion instruments—activate the spleen and base chakra centers of the body. These centers are linked to the functions of the circulatory system, the adrenals, and our basic life force. These are our centers of sexuality—the physical expression of our dynamic spiritual vitality.

Voudoun, (a Haitian religion) does not attempt to cloak or disguise its use of the drum for stimulating specific kinds of energies. Many of its rituals are utilized to block the rational mind out, to activate the sexual energies, and to induce trance. The incessant rhythmic drumming triggers a forced resonance with its energies.

Rhythms stimulate physical energy. Drumming can be a means of increasing blood flow throughout the body. The rhythms can quicken or slow the heartbeat and all organs associated with it. Thus, it was almost unthinkable for an ancient shaman, medicine person or healer not to have a drum or rhythm instrument. Depending upon the syncopation, or the pauses within the rhythms, specific physiological effects could be generated. In shamanic storytelling, the drum is used to bring the audience into resonance with each other and with the energies of the story. (This will be explored further in the chapter on "The Art of Magical Storytelling.")

Like its mate the drum, the rattle is one of the oldest healing instruments and is part of the percussion family. Unfortunately, its healing aspects are often ignored except by those who are interested in shamanism or traditional native healing processes. It has a versatility of healing through rhythms that other instruments do not. Also, because of its size, it is easily carried and transported.

The rattle and its rhythms have a capacity for linking the waking consciousness to the energies of the cosmos, or to levels of consciousness deep within. The inner levels of consciousness serve to release greater energy and power for the cleansing and healing process. The rattle is a *cleansing instrument*.

We are a bio-chemical/electro-magnetic energy system. Our thoughts and emotions trigger various frequencies of electro-magnetic impulses which interact with our bio-chemistry. Negative thoughts and emotions will set up rigid energy patterns within our auric fields. (This is much like the static or snowy picture on a T.V. that has poor reception.) These patterns are deviations from our true energy patterns and frequencies.

When we are in an environment in which negative thoughts and emotions predominate—whether of our own origin or not—they will impinge upon our individual energies and can bring us into resonance with them. If ignored or allowed to accumulate, they distort our basic life flow, and we become more susceptible to illness. These negative energy patterns usually lodge within the etheric body (that band of electro-magnetic energy surrounding and closest to the physical body) and within the chakra centers. If this static and negative energy debris is not cleaned out, any energy flowing to and through the physical body becomes sullied.

The etheric body is the filter for the physical, and the chakras mediate all energies coming into and flowing out of the physical. (See diagrams on "Mediation of Energy through the Chakras" in the next chapter.) It is important to keep those filters clean. Daily we connect with a tremendous amount of energy debris which can find resonance with our own energy and attach itself to us. Just as our water faucets can accumulate minerals and residues that prevent the free flow of water, so our own auric can become clogged with energy debris. The rattle is a rhythmic instrument that can shake loose any energy debris that has settled within our natural filters and mediators. It shakes loose the negative energy patterns, so they can be more easily cleansed from our entire energy field, physical and subtle. (Refer to the illustration "Shaking Up Negative Energy.")

The process is simple. The rattle is shaken while encircling the body. The rhythmic sounds of the rattle serve to loosen the rigid energy patterns that have accumulated within the etheric body. The rattle is then shaken while moving it up and down the central meridian of the body—usually front and back. This loosens up the energy debris that has attached itself and accumulated around or in the chakra centers. Some healers pause to give extra "shakes" at each chakra as these are places in the body in which there is a greater degree of electro-magnetic activity. Thus, they have a greater propensity for accumulating energy debris.

SHAKING UP NEGATIVE ENERGY

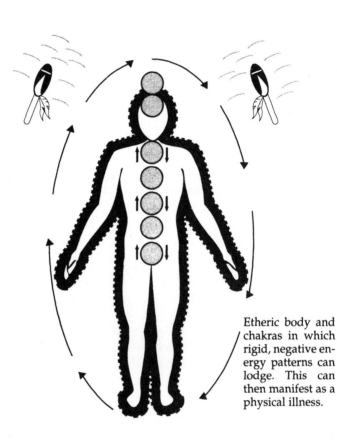

Etheric body and chakras in which rigid, negative energy patterns can lodge. This can then manifest as a physical illness.

The rattle is used in a variety of ways, depending upon the society and the illness. Regardless of the variation, there are some universal patterns to its use. The entire body is encircled. This loosens up negative energy patterns that have lodged within the etheric body. Then the rattle is shaken up and down over the body to loosen the energy within the chakras. This allows for easier cleansing of the negative energies—through other methods—by the practitioner.

Deciding which kind of rattle to use is an individual decision. Many rattles of the past were made from dried bones while others were made with seeds placed within a dried gourd. Many Native American and shamanic organizations sell rattles, so they are not only accessible but inexpensive as well. Also every person has the ability to use them without any previous musical knowledge. We can begin our own experiments with the rhythms of our energies.

Melody is the second aspect of the three-fold song of rhythm, melody, and harmony. From melody we can learn much about our relationships with other energies. Melody cannot exist without relationship. One tone by itself does not create a melody. As one tone is placed along side of other tones, melody is formed. Melody—whether, spoken, sung, or played upon an instrument—will soothe and alter emotional and mental states. It can balance mental stress and it can be used to relieve pain. Who has not seen a mother singing or humming softly to a crying child? (Often the mother rocks the child while doing so, and the rocking helps restore a soothing rhythm to the child's metabolism.) By singing to the child, the mother links her energies with those of the child (relationship), and the pain or emotion is soothed and balanced. In this way a gentle form of forced resonance is unconsciously employed.

Humming or singing a light melody throughout the day to that child that still lives within us is one of the most therapeutic things we can do for ourselves. It relieves stress and helps us to maintain balance.

Every melody is comprised of tones that do affect us on many levels. Here's a way to experience this: While on your way home from work, sing a simple childhood melody to yourself. This will restore balance and help to cleanse your energy of any negative debris you have accumulated within the work environment. More information on specific tones and their effects on us will be explored in the next chapter.

Hearing melody is one of the best ways to relax. The melody need only be light and simple. You do not have to be exposed to it for a great length of time for it to have an effect. Anyone who has ever sung or heard another sing a small child to sleep with a verse or two of "Brahms' Lullaby" understands this. If you do not believe that a simple melody has the power to affect people, go into work tomorrow, humming or whistling softly several rounds of "Pop, Goes the Weasel." Before the morning is over, you will be amazed at how many others have begun to sing or hum or whistle that same tune.

Harmony is the third part of the three-fold song. It is through harmony that the power of our own individual energy can link with the energy of the divine. In harmony lies not only a physical, emotional and mental aspect of sacred sound, but a spiritual aspect as well. When working with healing, the simpler the harmony the better. The relationship of one tone to another is reflected through harmony, as it is in melody.

A chord is two or more notes sounding simultaneously or arranged in accordance with harmonics. Ideally, the key tone is played, as are one or more of the overtones.[3] This blends the tones together to create a uniting of vibrations and power that one single tone could not create. Learning to blend the tones for various effects constitutes a study in itself. (Refer to Part Two: "The Art of Magical Storytelling.")

Working with harmony provides the key to transformation. It is the key to altering and transmuting, raising and lowering, adapting and shifting our energies and abilities on all levels. It enables us to transmute conditions of the physical body and alter our state of consciousness.

Like an alchemist, we turn the lead of our life into gold. By finding the right combinations of tones, rhythms, and harmonies, we can trigger a resonance within the body, mind, or soul so as to correct imbalances and to achieve higher states of consciousness.

This process reflects itself in all aspects of life. This is also readily apparent in the process of psychic unfoldment. As we work to develop one spiritual ability or psychic gift, others open up automatically and in harmony with the first. Those areas of expression compatible with our point of focus begin to unfold for us. We can call this the process of spiritual harmonics.

Although we are treating all three elements as distinct, they all have multiple functions. Yes, rhythm does affect the physical predominantly. Yes, melody affects the emotions and thoughts, as well as the body, and harmony affects us on all levels—physical, emotional, mental and spiritual. As we learn to employ each separately and then in combination, we begin to create the Three-Fold Song of the Absolute. We learn to mold and shape the energies through their combinations in creative and uniquely magical ways.

OTHER PRINCIPLES OF SACRED SOUND

The effects of sound—in any form—are cumulative and detectable.

The more we are exposed to beneficial sounds, the greater and the more permanent the effect they have upon our own individual energies. The more we are exposed to detrimental sounds, the greater the negative effect they have upon us on all levels.

Our bodies can discriminate between beneficial and detrimental sounds and will respond accordingly. These responses affect physical, emotional, mental and spiritual states. Unfortunately, most people do not recognize the effects until there is a physical response.[4] We can audibly detect when balance has occurred. Our voice is a great indicator, as we will discuss in the chapter on "The Occult Significance of Speech." We can audibly discern those sounds which are beneficial to us and those which are not. We must take into consideration individual tastes and needs, as we each have our own unique energy system.

Sound in any of its forms is a source of energy.

As a source of energy, it can be used to interact with other energies. Sound—whether through music, voice, or other sources—is effective as a tool to alter the electro-magnetic fields and impulses of an individual or an environment.

This means that if an imbalance has occurred within the body's normal electro-magnetic parameters (whether it is a dysfunction of a specific organ or of a particular system), we can utilize sacred sound in one of its forms or combinations to help restore homeostasis, alleviate pain or to accelerate healing.

As an energy source, it can also be used as a tool for the change of consciousness. It facilitates concentration, relaxation, learning, creativity and an increased awareness of psycho-spiritual states. It can interact with and help alter brain wave patterns to facilitate this process.

The PITCH of sacred sound in any of its forms must be considered in its effective application.

Pitch is the highness or lowness of the sound. The pitch is determined by the speed at which it vibrates. The faster the sound vibrates, the higher the pitch. Physically and spiritually, this tells us that as we raise our own individual energy levels we open to a higher degree of health. It is the raising of our energies to the highest pitch possible without unbalancing ourselves that is the task of the true student of life. It is a process that takes work. Rushing it is like taking gymnastics without preparations, there is a great possibility of injury occurring.

The principle of pitch tells us much about the evolution process. Low tones bend around objects when they are emitted. This is why in places where there is live band music, you will continue to hear the base and percussion instruments following after you as you leave the area. The low pitched tones bend around the corners and doorways. It is the path of least resistance.

High-pitched tones are more focused. Sometimes the absorption or resonance of high vibrations can be shattering to old forms. This is most easily demonstrated through the shattering of a crystalline glass by singing the properly pitched tone. It is also reflected in the changes that occur when someone encounters another of a highly intense energy field. It can shatter old concepts and habits—for good or for bad.

Working with pitch patterns can result in shattering rigid energy patterns that are limiting our growth, awareness and health. This shattering can manifest in some form of healing crisis, with a new perception and even an entirely new orientation to life.

The sacred sound aspect of pitch is that which can open us to higher energy levels in all aspects of our being. The higher and stronger our own energy fields are, the less likely they are to be impinged upon from outside sources, and the more we can adapt them to resonate to a wider spectrum of forces, people, and conditions of life.

In many ways we are like fans. We give off energy. With some people, the air is soft and weak and almost everything can pass through that air flow to affect the individual. With others the air is so strong that hardly anything can penetrate, and it can be adjusted to lower, less intense levels as needed.

We all have our own natural pitch, but there is also universal pitch. This is the ideal vibration. It is what will ultimately bring resonance with the divine. It will bring harmony with all life rhythms. We can use the pitches of instruments and voices to assist us in maintaining our own natural pitch while developing that link to the universal pitch. This will be explored in several of the processes discussed throughout this text.

How do you find your natural pitch at present? There are a number of ways. One of the easiest is by determining your vocal pitch. You will need to find a piano to assist you, or some instrument that can play several octaves of notes. Find the highest note that you can sing without your voice cracking. Then find the lowest note. The tone midway between the two is the pitch at which you are operating most at this time. As you work with many of the techniques explored in this text, re-check your pitch. You will find your range of pitches expanding—a wonderful growth indicator.

That tone which is midway is your strongest pitch of resonance at this time. In the sections to come, you can explore how to use it to facilitate your own growth and healing, through vocalizations, mantras, and instruments. Before we can employ sacred sound and the power of the Word to affect others, we must learn to apply it inwardly and affect ourselves first.

The TIMBRE of the sound in any of its forms must be considered in its effective application.

The quality, the distinctive characteristics, and the influence of sound is called timbre or tone color. It is the distinguishing source of all sound. It helps us to identify one sound from another, one voice from another, one instrument from another. Every sound and sound instrument has its own distinguishable characteristic.

It is timbre, along with pitch, which affects us most. Timbre creates responses that are either consonant or dissonant. Both terms relate to the energy perceptions toward outside stimuli and their resulting transformations.

When we respond with consonance to the timbre of various sounds—spoken or otherwise—we develop a positive rapport. The cells in our body recognize what sounds are good for us and respond accordingly. The timbre of fingernails across a blackboard is harsh and grating to the nervous system, while the timbre of a bamboo flute is soothing to the nervous system.

When we respond to sounds with dissonance, our energies and cells are distinguishing which sounds are not in harmony with us. Unless we pay attention to signals that our bodies give us, we may miss opportunities to enhance the beneficial effects or may allow the detrimental to impinge unnecessarily upon us.

Part of the secret power of the Word involves learning to control the timbre of the voice to create consonance or dissonance according to desires. Most of us do this naturally. If we wish to be left alone, we will assume a tone that is harsh or grating to others, pushing them away. If we wish to be friendly, we assume a tone of voice that is soft, gentle and light.

Through practice, we can learn to create physiological and spiritual changes in ourselves and others through altering the timbre of our speech and by employing the timbre of various instruments to elicit specific effects. The techniques and effects will be elaborated upon in the following chapters.

NOTES TO CHAPTER ONE

1. Air is the most common medium, but metal and
    water transmit sound vibrations more easily. Many
    ancient oracles and seers used water to increase their
    sensitivity to higher vibrations. Places of oracles
    were located near high cliffs (air) and underground
    caverns and lakes (the water and mineral media).
    Water was a common tool for prophecy and divina-
    tion. The water facilitated communication with ener-
    gies and beings of a higher vibration. Water in a
    metal container or cup was used as a divining instru-
    ment. Certain stones and metals also assisted in
    transmitting energies. This lead to the development
    and use of crystal balls, polished beryl, and dowsing
    rods as divination tools.

2. Although it cannot be historically verified and al-
    though there is no evidence that the lost continent of
    Atlantis ever existed, there have been many tales of
    this form of abuse associated with the Atlantean Ep-
    och. Many believe that during this time, it was recog-
    nized that each soul had its own individual keynote
    or tone. This tone was the key to restoring health and
    complete spirituality. The power of sacred sound,
    developed to a high degree within their temples,
    took the form of spoken song. They developed the
    ability to perceive the keynotes of individuals and
    natural objects. They then developed the ability to
    transmute physical conditions—to alter the physical
    vibrations—through those tones. Many believe it
    was the misuse of this knowledge that assisted in the
    collapse of this legendary civilization. Groups bent
    upon personal power instead of spiritual evolve-
    ment used techniques to discover the keynote of vari-

ous individuals. They would then direct a discordant variation of that tone at the individual to drive the ego from the physical. "Literally, blasts of tone, attuned to the keynote of a person or an object, were used to ruthlessly destroy human life and property."
— Corinne Heline, *Music: The Keynote of Human Evolution* (Santa Monica: New Age Bible Ctr, 1986) p. 35.

3. Almost every sound, musical or not, has overtones. (A sine wave does not have overtones, but it can only be created electronically, it does not occur naturally. These are vibrations set in motion at the same time as the primary tone. For example, if the note of middle C is struck upon the piano, the strings for the note of G above middle C, E, B-flat, etc. also begin to vibrate—although barely audibly. Four or five overtones are normally detectable and recognized in music, but theoretically the overtones extend much further than the human ear can detect. Thus, when we use music, sound, words, affirmation or prayers, we need to be aware that we are setting in motion overtones that will affect us as well. Those overtones are determined by the emotional and mental states of our energies. This is why we so often do not get what we are affirming or it manifests in an obtuse manner.

4. It has only been in the past 50 to 60 years that society as a whole has reached a decibel level in the 90 decibel range. Unfortunately, decibels increase their effects logarithmically. One decibel is the quietest sound that the average person can hear. Ten decibels of sound is ten times greater than one decibel, but 20 decibels is ten times greater than the ten decibel range or 100 times greater than one decibel. One hundred decibels is one billion times as intense as one decibel. Ninety decibels is equal to the sound of one

train pulling into a subway station. One hundred decibels is equal to the sound of ten trains pulling into the subway station simultaneously. One hundred and ten decibels is equal to the sound of one hundred trains pulling in.

CHAPTER TWO

The Magic
in Music

All sound and tone can fall into one of two categories—musical or non-musical. In this chapter we will explore the musical effects of sacred sound and how they can be applied by anyone, regardless of musical background or knowledge.

Everyone is musical. Everyone holds the gift of music within them. It is intrinsic to the nature of us all, without exception. We have been surrounded and nourished by music since the moment of conception—from the sounds carried to us through the amniotic fluids during pregnancy to the rhythmic beat of our own hearts. Music and rhythm are life itself.

Music is healing, and we must make it a conscious and active part of our lives. We must participate in music as we did as children. This is not just listening to it or using it to fill voids of silence in our lives. We must learn about it from an entirely new perspective. We must realize that within music lies all of the wonders and keys to the miracles of life. Within music lies all of the principles of life—natural and spiritual. Music can facilitate the process of change and growth.

It is recognized that a child responds to sound even while in the womb. The earth is our mother now—our womb—and we need to learn to work with the sounds of the earth much more creatively than in the past. You do not have to be "gifted" to benefit from work with sacred sound and music. Musicians are exceptional, but they are only "gifted" in the sense that they willingly and lovingly receive this gift which is available to all. They have taken what is part of us all, what is offered to us all, and then they have magnified it and made it their own. Even if we all can't be musicians, we all can be musical!

The consequences of higher consciousness and divine communication live on through music. When played, music will continue to pulse outward into the field of energy beyond us long after the actual sound has faded from audible awareness. Look how often we hear a tune in the morning, and we hum or hear it within our head throughout the rest of the day. This phenomenon says much about the spiritual and lasting effects of music. It even tells us that the possibility of communicating by music with the unseen is immeasurable.

Modern society views music in two ways, as an art form and as a commercial product. Music needs to be considered in a third way—*as a power of universal force*. It is a force that was treated with great respect in ancient times. They recognized that the physical emission of sound was an outer and audible agency of the inner transformation. They recognized that music was a relationship of one tone to another and that all life was the relationship of one individual to another.

The power of music works because of a secret content found in the expression of sound. This secret content is the pattern of sound emitted through various techniques, vocal or instrumental. For example, inspiration and intuition occurs through a repetition of regular musical structures, tones, and patterns that change the brain wave pattern from a beta (normal consciousness) to an alpha pattern (altered state of awareness).

Certain modes (minor and major) were deemed powerful. As a general rule, the minor modes were considered carriers of great force and power and could affect changes in emotional and physical states. The major modes were up uplifting and energizing. The minor mode draws the energy into the physical, and the major modes lift the individual to the spiritual.

The manner of playing and singing the modes was considered powerful. Some were literally banned by the Church. Many believed that the voice was wedded to words and that instruments lacked this unity. Many of the early church leaders also associated many instruments with pagan life. The lyre and flute, for example, were strongly associated with pagan dances.[1] Even though the lyre and flute were used in worship by the Greek converts to Christianity, the use of such instruments was condemned by such major figures as Clement of Alexandria, St. Ambrose, and St. Augustine[2] who "adjures believers not to turn hearts to theatrical instruments," even though Augustine exhorts the power of music and hymns.[3]

The Church often believed that Pagan musical instruments were derived from ancient magical practices that utilized music to invoke unseen beings and power. This was especially true regarding the singing of hymns. For example, in the development of singing polyphony, the interval of the minor second was prohibited.[4] And ecclesiastical authorities frowned upon the movement away from Gregorian Chants toward secular and possibly pagan melodies as a basis for the mass. In the traditional Greek music, (in the early chants and even in the folksongs) the text and the melody were united. However, individual singers who would adjust the text of the mass to fit with the music, using their own judgment, were condemned by the Council of Trent (1545-1563).[5]

The difficulty today in re-awakening much of the ancient knowledge and power of music lies in relating the old models to modern modes of awareness. The pitch ratio of ancient times would have to be tempered to today's world. Our own energy and expression is much different than that of thousands of years ago. When we apply the musical principles of the past to the present, it is not the individual notes that are of key importance, but rather it is the relationship of one tone to another.

Western society's scale is chromatic. It includes the basic eight notes from C to the next higher pitch of C (C, D, E, F, G, A, B, C). It also includes the sharps and flats in between them. On the piano this would constitute not only the white keys but the black keys as well.

Many ancient societies used a pentatonic scale—based upon five distinct notes. This is comparable to the five black keys on the piano. However, the black keys only represent one arrangement of the many possibilities in a pentatonic scale. Technically, any five notes can be considered a pentatonic scale.

EXAMPLE OF SCALES

Western Scales									Eastern Scales*					
Pentatonic	D	E	G A	B					Oriental	D	F	G A	C
Diatonic	C	D	E F	G A	B	(C)			African	D	E	G A	B
Chromatic	C	C# D	D# E	F F#					Egypt	F		G A	B C
	G	G# A	A# B	(C)					Greece	D	E	G A	B

*These are examples of pentatonic scales used in folksongs of these countries. There are others of course.

The tones associated with the scales give each society its own distinct sounds. This is why what sounds good to us in our society may sound quite discordant or strange to others, and vice versa. This is why westerners often dislike or don't understand many Eastern forms of music. It is not that the Eastern is discordant or inharmonious. It is simply based upon a different scale, a scale that is usually quite in harmony with the energies of that people. Each society—as each individual—has its own energy system. We in the West use our energies in ways that are quite different from those in the East. It is only natural that the expression of that energy through music would also be quite different.

It is not the number of notes within a particular scale that provides its force or impact, but rather it is the succession. The relationship between one note and the next provides the clue to the use of music for healing and for achieving higher states of consciousness. It is the order in which they are played, in conjunction with the rhythm, that creates the impact. Certain combinations of tones and rhythms have very specific effects upon our physical, emotional, mental, and spiritual states.

The order and rhythm of tones, and the mixing of tones into various melodies, is a source of magic. We can learn to combine tones—vocal or instrumental—to link energies of the body together. This can be done to facilitate healing, intuition, dream enlightenment, communing with spirits, or for invoking divine presences. We will explore a number of these techniques throughout this book.

HEALING ELEMENTS OF MUSIC

We can employ musical rhythms, tones, instruments, and vocalizations to interact with the various activities of the physiological systems of the body. The key to working with healing music is to understand how the chakra sys-

system relates to the physical and subtle aspects of our energies.

THE CHAKRA SYSTEM

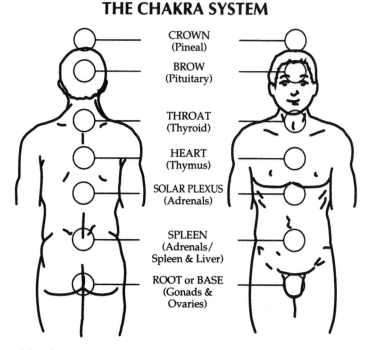

CROWN
(Pineal)

BROW
(Pituitary)

THROAT
(Thyroid)

HEART
(Thymus)

SOLAR PLEXUS
(Adrenals)

SPLEEN
(Adrenals/
Spleen & Liver)

ROOT or BASE
(Gonads &
Ovaries)

The electro-magnetic emanations of the body are strongest at the chakra points of the body. These emanations occur in front and in back of the body.

The chakras are the primary mediators of all energy already in the body and all energy coming into the body. They mediate the electro-magnetic impulses of our energy system. The chakras take the energy expressions and help the body distribute them for various physical, emotional, mental and spiritual functions. Although not part of the physical body, they link the subtle energy field that is surrounding the physical body to the activities of the body.

THE MEDIATION OF ENERGY THROUGH THE CHAKRA

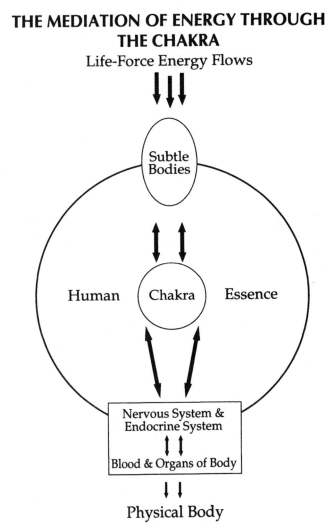

Life-Force Energy Flows

Subtle Bodies

Human   Chakra   Essence

Nervous System &
Endocrine System

Blood & Organs of Body

Physical Body

The normal life-force from each subtle body enters into its own particular chakra which then distributes the energy to the spinal contact, where it is in turn passed on to the blood stream and organs. When the food we eat is converted into energy, the process reverses itself so that the energy field and subtle bodies surrounding the physical are strengthened and energized.

BLOCKAGE OF THE FLOW OF ENERGY

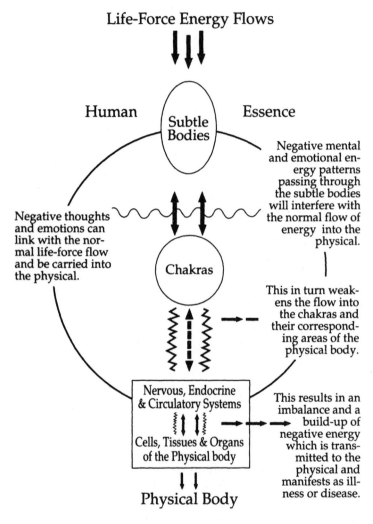

Life-Force Energy Flows

Human   Essence

Subtle Bodies

Negative mental and emotional energy patterns passing through the subtle bodies will interfere with the normal flow of energy into the physical.

Negative thoughts and emotions can link with the normal life-force flow and be carried into the physical.

Chakras

This in turn weakens the flow into the chakras and their corresponding areas of the physical body.

Nervous, Endocrine & Circulatory Systems

Cells, Tissues & Organs of the Physical body

This results in an imbalance and a build-up of negative energy which is transmitted to the physical and manifests as illness or disease.

Physical Body

The chakras are connected to the functions of the physical body primarily through the endocrine glands and the spinal system. They mediate the energy within and without the body through the various spinal contacts. Distribution occurs throughout the body by means of the nerve pathways and the circulatory system. In this way all of the organs, tissues, and cells receive the energy for their various uses. (Refer to the illustrations: "The Chakra System," "The Mediation of Energy Through the Chakra," and "Blockage of the Flow of Energy.")

Specific tones, rhythms, instruments, and vocalizations can be used to stimulate, balance and interact with the flow of electro-magnetic energies of the chakra system. Since they connect with the physical, we can use those same tones, rhythms, instruments and vocalizations to impact upon the corresponding physical organs and systems of the body itself.

Many times we fail to realize that the body knows how to take care of itself. Unfortunately, we do get in its way. We give it the wrong kinds of food. We overwork it. We don't allow it to rest. We expose it to stress and negativity. We hold on to emotions and attitudes that short circuit its energy flow, causing weaknesses and imbalances.

At times of imbalance, the chakras attempt to pull greater energy from our subtle bodies into the physical to counteract the dis-ease. If we are to correct the condition, we must first restore balance to our subtle energy system and to the natural flow of energy throughout the physical. In many cases, simply restoring the proper balance and functioning to the chakras will correct the imbalance, or at least alleviate it. Once the chakric energy flow is balanced, then the body can more easily concentrate on the physical manifestation of the dis-ease.

The most effective and simple means of restoring balance is through sound and music. The chakras and their electro-magnetic emanations respond to specific musical tones and vocalizations. If there is an imbalance, we can use specific tones or combinations of tones to restore homeostasis to the function of our electro-magnetic aspects.

The tones of our musical scale resonate with the seven major chakras of the body. Each chakra has its keynote. Tuning forks are effective for this, but they are also expensive. We can use a simple, inexpensive pitch pipe to balance the flow of energy of a particular chakra. We can sing an appropriate tone, or play it upon a musical instrument. We can also play a piece of music written in a key that is the primary tone for the imbalanced chakra. Many stores sell inexpensive synthesizers upon which we can play the tone or combinations of tones to help restore balance to a particular energy center and its physiological counterpart. (Refer to the illustration "Metaphysical Elements of Music.")

Certain tones and instruments can be used for balancing the chakra flow of energy. They can be used to restore physical, emotional, mental or spiritual balance. Sacred sound has physical as well as metaphysical properties. Imbalance within the energy of an individual may manifest through physical, emotional, mental or spiritual components. Thus, we must understand and examine the physical and metaphysical aspects of each chakra and their responses to sacred sound in any of its forms.

METAPHYSICAL ELEMENTS OF MUSIC

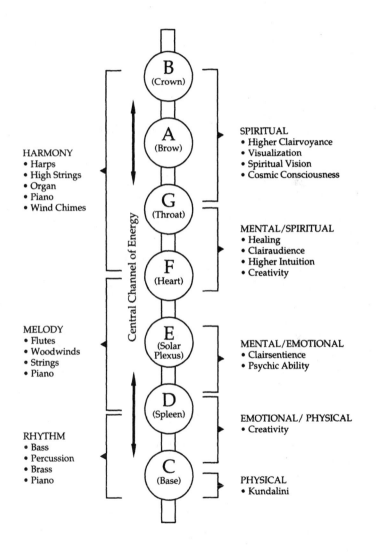

HARMONY
- Harps
- High Strings
- Organ
- Piano
- Wind Chimes

MELODY
- Flutes
- Woodwinds
- Strings
- Piano

RHYTHM
- Bass
- Percussion
- Brass
- Piano

Central Channel of Energy

B (Crown)

A (Brow)

G (Throat)

F (Heart)

E (Solar Plexus)

D (Spleen)

C (Base)

SPIRITUAL
- Higher Clairvoyance
- Visualization
- Spiritual Vision
- Cosmic Consciousness

MENTAL/SPIRITUAL
- Healing
- Clairaudience
- Higher Intuition
- Creativity

MENTAL/EMOTIONAL
- Clairsentience
- Psychic Ability

EMOTIONAL/ PHYSICAL
- Creativity

PHYSICAL
- Kundalini

MUSICAL INTERPLAY WITH THE CHAKRAS

Base Chakra

Sacred Sounds that Balance and Stimulate
- Tone of middle C.
- Bass and percussion instruments.
- Long U vowel sound.

Physical Aspects
It is located at the area of the coccyx at the base of the spine. It is tied to the functions of the circulatory system, the reproductive system, and the functions of the lower extremities. It is our basic life-force center. It influences the activities of the testicles and ovaries, the legs and feet and the pelvis area of the body.

Metaphysical Aspects
This is our center for life-promoting energy. Stimulated properly, it can open an awareness of past life talents and ease fears. It is the seat of the kundalini within the body.

Emotional/Mental Attitudes Causing or Reflecting Dysfunction
Reactive; aggressive; belligerent; manipulative; impulsive; reckless; inability to recognize limits; abrupt; domineering; craving excitement; possessive and territorial; needing approval; acting without thinking; power conscious; constantly active (hyperactive); reluctant to defer gratification; bullying; obsessively sexual.

Spleen Chakra

Sacred Sounds that Balance and Stimulate
- Tone of D above middle C.
- Bass, percussion, brass, and woodwind instruments.
- Long O vowel sound.

Physical Aspects

This center is tied to the function of the adrenal glands partially. It is also a major influence on the reproductive system and the entire muscular system of the body. It influences the eliminative system, the activities of the spleen, bladder, pancreas, and kidneys. It is a major center influencing the detoxification of the body.

Metaphysical Aspects

This is a center influencing sensation and emotion. It is tied to the consciousness of creativity. It is a center which controls most personality functions, and it can be stimulated to open one to communication with energies and beings upon the astral plane.

*Emotional/Mental Attitudes Causing
or Reflecting Dysfunction*

Selfishly arrogant; lustful; proud; conceited; vain; mistrustful of others; following the crowd; worrying what others think; unable to get along with others; valuing social status; expansive without substance; power-seeking; anti-social.

Solar Plexus Chakra

Sacred Sounds that Balance and Stimulate
- Tone of E above middle C.
- Flutes, woodwinds, strings, and piano instruments.
- Vowel sound of "awh."

Physical Aspects
This center is linked to the solar plexus area of the physical body. This includes the digestive system, the adrenals, the stomach, the liver, and the gall bladder. It assists the body in its assimilation of nutrients. It is also linked to the functions of the left hemisphere of the brain. Many crippling diseases, ulcers, intestinal problems, and psychosomatic diseases are eased by working with this center.

Metaphysical Aspects
This center is tied to the function of clairsentience and general psychic energies and experiences. It also has links to the rational thought processes. When activated for non-physical purposes, it can reveal the talents and capacities of other souls. It can open our attunement to the influence of nature's elements.

Emotional/Mental Attitudes Causing or Reflecting Dysfunction
Feeling deprived of recognition; aloof; dogmatic; opinionated; fearing group power; isolating; confining life to a narrow view; always planning but never manifesting; constantly needing change and novelty; judgmental; critical; mentally bullying; feeling self is unerring; absolutist in attitude.

Heart Chakra

Sacred Sounds that Balance and Stimulate
- Tone of F above middle C.
- Harps, organs, flutes, wind chimes and all string instruments.
- Long A vowel sound.

Physical Aspects
The heart chakra is influential in the function of the thymus gland and the entire immune system. It is tied to the functions of the heart itself and the circulatory system of the body. It affects the assimilation of all nutrients and it is tied to all heart and childhood diseases. It is linked to the right hemisphere of the brain and its processes. It is also tied to the process of tissue regeneration.

Metaphysical Aspects
This is the mediating center of the chakras. It is the center that awakens compassion and its expression in our lives. It is our center for expressing higher love and healing energies. If stimulated properly, it opens our sight of the deeper forces in plants and animals. It awakens knowledge of the sentiments and dispositions of others as well.

Emotional/Mental Attitudes Causing or Reflecting Dysfunction
Angry; always expecting confirmation from others; inability to enforce own will; financially insecure; emotionally insecure; uncertain; miserly; wanting to possess love; needing recognition from others; focused only on self; possessive; jealous and envious; self-doubting; always blaming others; mistrustful of life.

Throat Chakra

Sacred Sounds that Balance and Stimulate
- Tone of G above middle C.
- Harps, organs, pianos, and high string instruments.
- Vowel sounds of short E, I, U, & A (eh, ih, uh, ah).

Physical Aspects
The throat chakra is tied to the functions of the throat, the esophagus, the mouth and teeth, the thyroid and the parathyroid glands. It is influential in the functions of the respiratory system, the functions of the bronchial and vocal apparatus. The alimentary canal is also part of its area of influence.

Metaphysical Aspects
This center is tied to the functions of the right hemisphere of the brain and the creative functions of the mind. It can be stimulated to open one to clairaudience and to manifest greater abundance. It can be stimulated so as to survey the thoughts of others (telepathy), and it opens the consciousness to insights into the true laws of natural phenomena.

Emotional/Mental Attitudes Causing or Reflecting Dysfunction
Seeking dominion over others; surrendering to superiors constantly; trapped by fixed ideas; clinging to tradition; always needing rules and supervision; being smug and self-satisfied; rigidly dogmatic; resisting change; melancholic; fanatical; rigid and stubborn; authoritarian; being slow to respond.

Brow Chakra

Sacred Sounds that Balance and Stimulate
- Tone of A above middle C.
- Harps, organs, pianos, wind chimes, and high string instruments.
- Long E vowel sound.

Physical Aspects
The brow chakra influences the functions of the pituitary gland and the entire endocrine system of the body. It also has links to the immune system as well. It affects the synapses of the brain. It is a balancing center for the functions of the hemispheres of the brain. It is linked to the sinuses, eyes, ears and the face in general.

Metaphysical Aspects
This is the center for higher clairvoyance and the entire magnetism of the body (the feminine aspects of our energies). It opens one to higher and clearer perceptions. It is intricate in the process of imagination and creative visualization. It can open one to spiritual vision.

Emotional/Mental Attitudes Causing or Reflecting Dysfunction
Worrying; fearful of the unconscious; fascinated with external intelligence; seeking power for selfish reasons; pursuing idolized relationships; envious of other's talents; impatient; late for appointments; superstitious; inefficient; unable to live in the now; "spaced out;" forgetful; fearful of the future; undisciplined; introverted; belittling of others; oversensitive to impressions of others; unable to manifest.

Crown Chakra

Sacred Sounds that Balance and Stimulate
- Tone of B above middle C.
- Harps, organs, pianos, wind chimes, and high string instruments.
- Long E vowel sounds.

Physical Aspects
The crown chakra is tied to the functions of the nervous system and the entire skeletal system of the body. It influences the pineal gland, all nerve pathways and electrical synapses within the body. It is also linked to the balanced functioning of the hemispheres of the brain.

Metaphysical Aspects
This chakra is the link to our spiritual essence. It aligns us with the higher forces of the universe; it is powerful in the purification of our subtle bodies, especially in preparing them as separate vehicles of consciousness. It can open you to all of your past lives and how they have led to this point within the present incarnation. It is critical to integrating your spiritual self with your physical self within the circumstances of your present life.

Emotional/Mental Attitudes Causing
or Reflecting Dysfunction
Feeling misunderstood; Unable to have enduring relationships at deep levels; having intense erotic imaginations; using power to overwhelm others; needing sympathy; critical; feeling shame, self-denial and self-abasement; having a negative self image; daydreamy; needing to feel popular or indispensable; not understanding need for tenderness.

TONAL AND SPINAL CONTACTS OF CHAKRAS

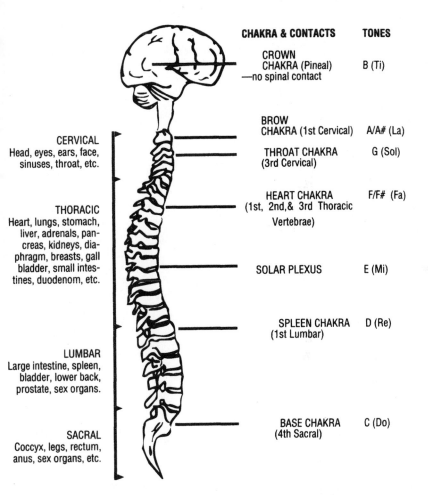

Vibrations—whether through tones, sounds, or colors—enter through the chakras. They balance the flow of energy within the chakras and this balanced vibration is then transmitted into the vertebrae of the spine. The vertebrae are extremely strong sound resonators, and they pick up the sound vibrations and transfer them along the nerve pathways to the organs and tissues.

PROVING THE EFFECTS

Two of the most enjoyable aspects of my seminars on healing with sound, music, and voice is the demonstration of (1) how easy it is to short circuit the energy system of the body through emotions and attitudes and (2) how easy it is to restore that balanced flow of energy through tones—instrumental or vocal. The most effective way of demonstrating these aspects is through kinesiology.

Kinesiology is the study of the muscular movements in the body—voluntary and involuntary—and their interactions with the rest of the body. Part of its study is the connection between the muscles and the electrical system of the body. As the muscles move, electrical energy is released. "The term 'kinesthesia' means conscious recognition of the orientation of different parts of the body with respect to each other as well as the rates of movement of the different parts of the body. These functions are subserved principally by extensive sensory endings in the joint capsules and ligaments ... These endings are stimulated strongly when the joint is suddenly moved; they adapt slightly at first but then transmit a steady signal thereafter."[6]

Our thoughts put out brain wave patterns—electromagnetic frequencies—that can easily interfere with the functioning of the muscles and the entire electrical system of the body. Too much negative energy will weaken the muscles. If we make contact with a weakened area to test it, it will lose energy and become weaker.

This is the purpose of muscle testing. It provides a feedback system that lets us know how outside energies, including our own emotions and thoughts, are affecting our physiological processes. Muscle testing is simple and it helps develop a body awareness. It is a way of providing ourselves with feedback about the functions of our energies. It does have some limitations.

A common limitation that some may notice is the influence of personal expectation and suggestion. They play a part, but remember that our thoughts and emotions do affect physiological conditions and processes of the body. We are simply trying to develop a heightened awareness of them.

A second limitation is that of the muscles on the upper and lower arms cancelling out their strengths. However, we are simply working to establish a relationship between the chakra and the physiological response. We do this by isolating and focusing upon one predominant muscle. Muscles do not work alone, and because of this one muscle on its own is not going to be as strong. This is also why we test only the first couple inches of range in the muscle action. Because of the kinesthetic action, the muscle will be either test strong in the first part of the test or will give completely.

It is a good idea to first test for general strength, to get a feel for the muscle's strength, then retest it after short-circuiting it by focusing upon a particular thought or emotion. Then test it yet a third time after the sound treatment is applied. Fatigue does not play a part, as the test only takes several seconds and there is an interval of rest between the tests.

The first testing procedure will involve another person. It is a process I use in workshops to allow participants to experience the effects more personally:

1. Choose a chakra center to test. (If you wish you can test them all, and it is beneficial to do so on a daily basis. It does not take much time, and it prevents imbalances from getting a foothold in manifesting a physical dis-ease.) You will be testing the general

strength of the chakra, as well as the functions associated with it.

2. Have the individual to be tested extend his/her dominant arm out to the side. (If you are right-handed, that is your dominant arm; if you are left-handed, that will be your dominant arm.) Have them place their other hand on the chakra point to be tested.

3. As you apply gentle pressure to the upper part of their arm, attempt to push the individual's arm down, while he/she resists. Tell him/her to prevent you from pushing the arm down, if he/she can. Test only the first couple of inches of range, applying the pressure gradually and releasing it gradually. Use a gentle, yet firm pressure. The muscle will either be strong in the first part of the test, locking in place, or it will give way. If it gives way, follow through with the movement. Learn to attune to the strength and resistance. Does the arm lock or does it feel mushy?

4. Having determined the general and present strength of the chakra, it is time to demonstrate how to short-circuit its function. We will use the heart chakra for this test. After the initial testing of strength, have the individual return both arms to his/her side, close the eyes and think back on the last thing that really irritated or angered him/her. Anger is an emotion that will cause or reflect imbalance within the functioning of the heart chakra.

5. When the individual has brought the incident to mind, have him/her extend the arm once more, placing the other hand upon the heart center. Ask him/her to resist as strongly as possible as you test its

strength a second time. You will find the muscle response will be noticeably weaker, demonstrating that emotions will short-circuit our systems.

This is why it is important to be aware of the range of emotions you are exposed to throughout the day, as they can short-circuit your chakra system, resulting in imbalances that can lead to physical illnesses.

6. Having shown the weakness, it is now most important to demonstrate how sacred sound can be employed to restore homeostasis to the chakra functioning. I use a tuning fork in the workshop demonstration, but you can also tone the vowel sound for the chakra, projecting it at that particular center. In this case we would tone the vowel of long A. (This process of directed esoteric toning to restore balance will be elaborated upon in the next chapter.) You can also use a pitch pipe, and play the appropriate tone three to five times.

If you have another musical instrument, you can also play the appropriate tone upon it, and the results will be the same. As we now know, certain musical instruments will also balance and stimulate the chakra centers. Playing a piece of music with the appropriate instrument can restore the balance. For example, if you are balancing the solar plexus center, play a recorded piece of music that has flutes featured predominantly. In my workshops, I take about thirty to sixty seconds and play a bamboo flute to show how little it takes to restore the chakra to its normal strength. At the end of this chapter is a list of simple restoration techniques that can be applied to any or all of the chakras.

7. The next step, after applying the sacred sound, is to test the strength a third time. You will find it as strong as the first test or even stronger. It is always important to retest to check the effectiveness of the treatment.

8. You can also test yourself. You can use the fluidity of arm movement—up and down. The more fluid the range of motion, the stronger and more balanced each chakra is. You can also use the thumb and first finger, holding them together in a circle. As you focus on the chakra, use the thumb and first finger of your other hand to try and separate the fingers on the dominant hand. This gives you some physical clues to the strength and functioning of the chakra system of your own body. There are books in the library and in most health stores that explore other techniques of muscle testing to give yourself more feedback.

MUSIC OF ASTROLOGY

The ancient Egyptians, from whom the Greeks derived many of their mathematical and musical concepts, recognized that the universe lived in perfect harmony. The solar system has its own octave that vibrates in harmony with all other solar systems in the universe. Each planet within the solar system has its own distinct tone that is part of that octave. Together, the planets form a composition.

There have been many individuals in the past who have related the planets and the signs of the zodiac to music.[7] While many have done this by simply ranking them and assigning a corresponding pitch (the total comprising the musical scale), Pythagorus based it upon mathematics and relative distances.[8] Other tonal associations have been based upon colors and days of the week.[9] Yet other tonal associations were based upon the motions of the planets. Different pitches were assigned for different rates of revolution.[10]

Just as with the planets, the signs of the zodiac have also had musical tones assigned to them in the past. Foremost of those who worked with the tonal zodiacs were Ptolemy,[11] Johannes Keppler[12] and others of different esoteric orders. A tonal correspondence zodiac based on the work of Rosicrucian teacher Max Heindel is depicted in the "Music of the Spheres: Wheel Two" illustration.[13] Others though have also made their own correspondences. Rudolph Steiner promoted a tonal zodiac based upon tonal fifths. This is still strong in the Anthroposophical teachings today.[14]

Although the correspondences may seem arbitrary at times, for the modern spiritual student, it is important to breathe as much significance into whatever system is employed. In this way, the associations become a tool to assist in the developing of growth and perception beyond the tangible. For example, the tonal correspondences in the in the "Music of the Spheres: Wheel One" illustration is based upon the chromatic scale, beginning with middle C. It relates these tones in the order normally associated with the various signs of the zodiac. Thus middle C becomes Aries, C–sharp becomes Taurus, etc. Whatever system of tones is used, for their greatest magical application the individual must develop his or her own significances and associations with them.

When we were born, the stars and planets were in a particular position within the universe. The tones and harmonies of these heavenly bodies at the time you were born are also living within you. The position of the stars and planets hold the patterns of our strongest potentials and our greatest learnings. Working with them and bringing them into harmony and symphony with our own lives is an aspect of alchemy. We are aligning our individual energies to more universal expressions. Through music, we can come to understand how those astrological energies affect us.

As we have seen, every sign of the zodiac and every planet has a particular vibration or musical tone that can be associated with it. It is the relationship that you build between the various tones and the planets that determines how strong their significance is. Astrology and music are tools to help us to understand the energies within us and how to bring them into harmony.

Using either method, it is possible to transpose the astrological chart of an individual into a musical composition. All of us have the capacity to recognize what sounds good to us and what does not. When the astrological chart is transposed into a musical composition, we can hear what is harmonious and what isn't. Those parts of the astrological symphony which sound more discordant will indicate areas in which you need to work for greater harmony. This does imply some creative work on the part of the individual.

In the astrological symphony, the aspects or relationships of the planets become chords, two or three notes played in unison. Ideally, these tones or planets enhance and blend well with each other, but musically, we know that some tones sound very discordant when played with others. If a discordant aspect is found within an astrological chart, we can play various musical tones that blend well with that aspect, bringing harmony into the disharmony.

For example, the aspect referred to as an opposition indicates any two or more planets that are 180 degrees apart from each other. In this relationship, they oppose

MUSIC OF THE SPHERES:
WHEEL ONE

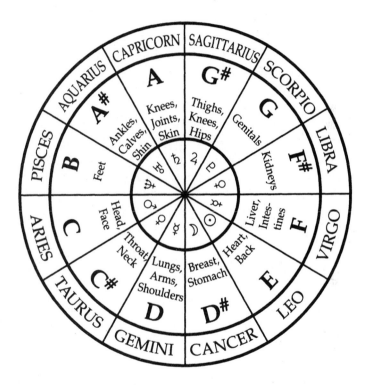

Astrologically, specific tones can be linked to the signs and the planets and the corresponding parts of the body.

The chart can be converted into a composite that reflects the energies with which the individual incarnated.

MUSIC OF THE SPHERES:
WHEEL TWO

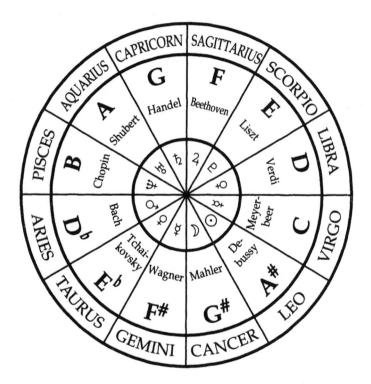

Through astrological symphony, one can determine what to emphasize and what to work on in their life process. This wheel can be used to create a musical composition that will provide balance, harmony and higher consciousness through combinations of tones—linked and correlated to the individual's own astrological chart. This wheel is based on tonal correspondences developed by Max Heindel.

each other or are on opposite sides of the astrological chart. Johannes Kepler established correlations between astrological aspects and consonances of music, based upon their mathematical relationships. A trine, for example, is an aspect in which the planets are 120 degrees apart. This gives it a ratio of 360:240 or 3:2. This is the mathematical ratio for the musical interval of a perfect fifth.[15]

We all have encountered people to whom we are seemingly in complete opposition. In astrology, this represents energies that oppose, resist or block us. How much opposition exists can be determined musically by the blending of the tones. Finding a tone to soften the discordant sound or finding the tone(s) that work best with each separate planet enables us to recognize where the focus of our energies needs to be placed to transmute the condition.

Using the wheel in the "Music of the Spheres: Wheel One" illustration, an opposition between the Sun and Moon could be represented by the tones of E for the Sun and D-sharp for the Moon.[16] These two tones when played together sound discordant. This particular opposition may indicate difficulty in harmonizing the inner and outer parts of ourselves. By playing around with the tones, we can find several ways of doing this:

1. Emphasize the Mercury energies of the chart. If there is to be an outer expression of the self (Sun), let it be through communication. Mercury has a tone of F which is more harmonious with the moon tone of D-sharp. This would also indicate a need to communicate and bring out the internal (Moon) feelings through various forms of communication. Care would need to be taken to not internalize all feelings and thoughts.

2. Another method of using the music to bring harmony to this opposition would be by emphasizing

Jupiter and Neptune energies, the tones associated with G-sharp and B. When played with the tones of the sun and moon, they create an E7 chord. The energies of the chart associated with all four of these planets harmonize well together, manifesting a positive expression of energy so that the sun and moon would not block each other.

The potential within musical astrology is infinite. Solar returns can be transposed to let you audibly hear the changes in the coming year. We can learn to blend all elements of the chart. The healing potential alone is magnificent. Healing temples could be formed in which groups of healers, those associated with or capable of intoning sounds for each sign of the zodiac or planet, could encircle the individual. Through the use of specific combinations of tones, balance could be restored to the body and soul.

To hear one's astrological chart played musically is at once eerie and awesome. Musically, it resonates deep within us. To meditate with it releases tremendous insight and results in the achievement of higher states of consciousness. It touches depths of the soul previously unrecognized. Its potential is as unlimited as we are unlimited.

INDIVIDUAL METHODS FOR EMPLOYING MUSICAL EFFECTS

1. Employ the appropriate tone for the chakras:
   — through singing the tone (Do, Re, Mi...).
   — through playing a piece of music written in the key appropriate to the chakra. (Libraries are excellent sources for finding appropriate classical music in the appropriate key.)
   — through the use of an instrument, either playing it or playing a recording of it.

— by playing an inexpensive pitch pipe and using the tones from it.

— through synthesized music (many inexpensive synthesizers are currently on the market).

— through the process of directed esoteric toning, using vowel sounds as described in the following chapter.

— through learning to play a musical instrument. It is never too late, and there are instruments that are relatively easy to acquire and to learn. Recorders and bamboo flutes are but one example.

2. One of the most effective melodies that you can employ to balance and heal yourself regularly is through a simple song that most children can sing. It is the "Do, Re, Mi..." song: "Do, a deer, a female deer. Re, a drop of golden sun..." This song from the musical *The Sound of Music* has great healing capabilities. It employs the whole octave, affecting every chakra. It also has a pumping action in its rhythm that activates and pulls the energy up from the base and activates the upper centers as well.

Singing its verses through three to four rounds is cleansing to the auric field. It balances and aligns the chakras. It relieves emotional and mental stress. When sung first thing in the morning, it pulls us into alignment with the physical body so that it doesn't take until almost noon to wake up.

When singing this song, especially in the morning, the first two rounds may sound a bit rough, but by the time you are on your third or fourth round, you will notice how much better and more "wonderful" your singing is sounding. This is an audible clue that you are becoming balanced and coming back into alignment.

NOTES TO CHAPTER TWO

1. Erwin Esser Nemmers, *Twenty Centuries of Catholic Music* (Milwaukee: Bruce Publishing, 1949) p. 5.

2. Edward Dickinson, *Music in the History of the Western Church* (New York: Charles Scribners, 1902) p. 54–55.

3. St. Augustine *Confessions* (trans. R. S. Pine-Coffin (New York: Dorset Press, 1961) Book IX, chapters 6, 7.

4. Ibid., 92–93.

5. Ibid., Pages 109–111.

6. Arthur C. Guyton, M.D. *Basic Human Physiology* (Philadelphia: W.B. Saunders Company, 1971), p. 397.

7. Joscelyn Godwin, *Harmonies of Heaven and Earth* (Rochester: Traditions International, 1987), pp. 125–152.

8. Pliney, *Natural History*, II, trans. H. Rackman (Cambridge: Harvard University Press, 1979), p. 19.

9. H.P. Blavatsky, *The Esoteric Writings of H.P. Blavatsky* (Wheaton: Quest Books, 1980) p. 360–370.

10. Macrobius, *Commentary on Dream of Scipio*, trans. William Harris Stahl; (New York: Columbia University Press, 1951), p. 73.

11. Ptolemy, *Harmonics* (New York: Garland Press, 1980), Vol. III, p. 8. This association of notes is also discussed by Ernest McClain in his book *The Pythagorean Plato* (New York: Nicholas Hays, 1978) p. 151.

12. Johannes Kepler "Harmonies of the World: V," trans. Charles Glenn Wallis. *Encyclopedia Brittanica's Great Books of the Western World: 16—Ptolemy, Copernicus and Kepler* (Chicago: 1952) pp. 1026–1048.

13. Max Heindel, *The Musical Scale and the Scheme of Evolution* (Oceanside: Rosicrucian Fellowship, 1970), p. 36.

14. Ernst Hagemann, ed. and trans. *Rudolph Steiner, Vom Wesen Des Musikalischen* (Freiburg: Die Kommenden, 1974), p. 93.

15. Joscelyn Godwin *Harmonies of Heaven and Earth* (Rochester: Inner Traditions International, 1987), pp. 148–149.

16. In the discussion of the tones for the chakras, the heart center—the sun center for the body—is represented by the tone of F. This differs from the astrological tone for the sun. The difference is insignificant. E is only one half of an interval from F. They are both within or close to the same frequency. There are, of course, differences, but these are only guidelines. They are tools to assist us in our growth.

CHAPTER THREE

The Occult Significance of Speech

Language, and the words and sounds that comprise it, is poorly understood. Misconceptions abound. It is presumptuous of humanity to think that its nature is self-evident, or that we know all that we need to know simply because we speak it. Philosophers have always been greatly interested in it and its psychological connections to humanity. Language and its expression is of central importance to understanding our thought processes. It is critical to realizing our spiritual aspects and how those spiritual aspects interplay with our life on physical levels. Linguistics is the study of language, but there is also what could be termed metaphysical linguistics—how language affects us beyond the physical realms.

The study of language and its uses has a long and ancient history. It is generally believed and accepted that most of our modern languages stem from forms of the Sanskrit language. Sanskrit in and of itself is dead, but Indian yogis still use Sanskrit words and sounds because of their sonorous effects to enhance their meditations. The languages of many ancient traditions and rituals are still considered sacred, and any changes in the words or their pronunciations is felt to threaten the inherent power of those words. What the ancient mystery traditions had in common was the recognition of the power of language and spoken words. Knowing the real name of a being is still believed by many to give the possessor of this knowledge a certain power over that being.

The ancient teachers and masters used symbology to communicate many of their teachings. They recognized the power of words and languages. Words were precisely selected by the teacher. Pythagoras, for example, was a great teacher and there are many stories about his teaching methods. He wore masks so that his students would be influenced by the words themselves and not by his facial expressions. In this way, the symbology of the language had to be searched out and understood individually.

The ancient teachers knew that certain words attracted blessings, gave power, brought release from illness, instilled courage, strength and comfort. Events and lessons were recorded symbolically. The student was not allowed to recite religious or historical events, traditions or legends lest the powers associated with them would be invoked and brought again into manifestation. The oral traditions and legends were recited only at holy times— times of sacred festivals and initiation. The student had the responsibility of translating them into his or her own symbolic interpretation and working with it. The symbology of the student is what would ultimately be tested by the master to ensure the student had achieved proper depth of meaning and significance.

Sacred sounds and words were imparted carefully to the student of the mysteries. The disciples had to first prove their selflessness and love for humanity. They had to become educated in the mystical and metaphysical arts to the degree that they could unfold their lower and higher minds and link them with a bridge (a bridge often based upon the power of words and language). They had to graduate from tests of silence. They had to learn how to speak, what to speak and most importantly, when to speak if they wished the higher knowledge of sounds and words.

Those who sought to learn the occult significance of language and the power of words had to first unlearn their previous use of words and refrain from "ordinary" methods of talking. In the Pythagorean schools of wisdom, the neophytes were not to speak for their first five years.[1] This was done to help them learn reticence of speech. They had to develop the ability to maintain silence so as not to reveal secrets through words or thought processes. The concept of strength through silence was a living, working reality.

Just as music is played externally but realized within, so it is with words and language. Words and their sounds vibrate to different parts of the body, different chakras, different organs, different emotional and mental states, and different states of consciousness. Some have power over the physical, and some can quicken the emotions. To a great degree, the power of words depends upon the depth from which the word arises and how illuminated the individual is that uses it. This is why some individual's words will penetrate into our hearts as if spoken in tongues of flame, while others may say the same thing a hundred times and it still does not penetrate.

Our minds are reflectors of words. We can build barriers to many things we do not wish to hear and even to those things we do. Yes, the word has power, but it is not just what we say, it is also how we feel, how we express it and the purpose behind the expression.

We have all experienced the power of language. We say something humorous and we laugh. We say something sad and we cry. Everyday in commercials and advertisements, we experience the power of words and language. Wall Street and the advertising industry has created a new form of mass "word magic." Language is used to manipulate our energies, emotions, and ideas. They have learned to penetrate any mental deflectors we may put up. We are a society obsessed with the idea that being young and thin is the only path to happiness. Those within the advertising field have learned to utilize words of ordinary speech to create tremendous effects. If they can do this with our ordinary words, imagine what WE could do with the ancient mystical words and sounds which carry even greater force and power!

Language is a magical force and speech is its vehicle. It works intimately with the laws of manifestation. The ancient magicians knew how to manifest through the powers of speech and silence. They knew how to employ language to open the doors between humanity and subtle beings. They knew how to use language to pass through the veil that separates the physical from the other dimensions and realities. Helena Blavatsky's book *The Secret Doctrine* defines magic as addressing the gods in their own language. It is this that we all can learn to do.

Language and thought occur independently, and yet there is an intimate relationship. Our thoughts operate with a very fine form of energy, one that can not be easily discerned in the physical realm. It sets the matrix of energy that we are wishing to manifest. Through speech, that matrix of energy is intensified and introduced into the physical realms of energy. It is brought out of that abstract, ethereal realm and becomes grounded into the physical, where it will manifest.

The subconscious mind controls 90 percent of our body's activities and functions. It also responds in a literal manner to every thought and word. It takes every thought and word and uses them as clues to working and handling our energies and their expressions within our lives. When we tell ourselves or others that we catch two colds every winter, the subconscious mind immediately begin working on the energies of your body, so that as winter approaches, we become more susceptible to "catching" those two colds. Our words and thoughts can become self-fulfilling prophecies. The more we think about something and the more we say something in conjunction with that thought, the stronger and quicker that energy will manifest within our physical lives.

We are multi-dimensional, and our words must reflect that.

All energy follows thought. When we give those thoughts vocalization, that energy is given great impulse toward manifesting. If we tell ourselves that we are clumsy or uncreative, then we see circumstances which prove it to us. We say to ourselves, "That's so stupid of me" or "That's unbelievable" and then we wonder why things do not work out for us. We criticize ourselves, mentally and verbally, and then we are upset when our lives are confused and ineffective.

There are always some people who say that they can't help how they think of themselves. They say its ingrained. That's how they were treated as a child. If so, that is sad, but if we continue those same patterns ourselves, then it is sadder still.

The past cannot be changed, but the future is being shaped by our current thoughts and words. When we emit words that relate to our thoughts—positive or negative—we are releasing that mental energy matrix into our physical lives.

THE POWER OF VOICE CONSCIOUSNESS

There is a strong correlation between our thoughts, our voice, and breath. Through voice and breath, the mental energy created by our thoughts can be given manifestation within our lives. Voice is a manifestation of breath, and breath is life itself while we are within the physical. Breath is audible. It is a word itself. It is the life behind the words.

Our voice is our most creative and musical instrument. It has great power to touch our lives and the lives of others. With our voice and the words we use, we can lighten another's load. We can help someone to feel as if they are walking in God's shadow. We can also use our voice to cut the legs out from others and make them feel as if their life was a living Hell.

The more we learn to link the use of breath, mind, and voice, the greater our own power in life. As we increase our awareness of their power, and as we learn to control their use, we open ourselves to worlds that once were merely the product of an overly active imagination.

The ancient Greeks raised the question of whether there is something special in the relationship of a word and the thing which it represents or whether the relationship was arbitrary. They raised the question as to whether the sounds of the words carried the meaning or whether the meaning was already inherent, regardless of vocalization. And what, if anything, did this have to do with our voice? Plato decided that "names belong to things by nature . . . and an artisan of words is he who keeps in view the name which belongs by nature to each particular thing." (Plato speaks of the nature of names extensively in his dialogue, *Cratylus*.)

The voice is an expression of our spirit and character. There is an interrelationship between the five elements of nature and the voice itself. The voice reflects one of the five elements or combinations. These elements also reflect the plane or dimension from which the individual derives much of his or her innate energy. Becoming a Master of the Word involves learning to use all of these voices, singly or in combination, in a fully conscious manner.

THE ELEMENTS AND VOICE QUALITIES

Element	Voice Quality	Source Of Energy
Earth	hopeful, encouraging, tempting	physical/etheric
Water	soothing, healing, intoxicating	astral / physical
Air	uplifting, calming, detached	mental/all below
Fire	arousing, exciting, frightening	spiritual & below
Ether	inspiring, healing, harmonizing	spiritual

These qualities are subjective. No hard and fast definitions can be given to them. Just as music has the qualities of pitch, volume, and timbre, so does the human voice. It is the timbre and pitch of the voice that determines its elemental relationship. We change our voice to suit our purposes. If we wish to be soothing, we take on a gentler tone. If we wish to strengthen and encourage, we take a tone of voice that is steady and firm. Learning to work with the power of the Word requires we learn to do this shifting of vocalizations consciously and selectively.

The degree of resonance determines which element is most closely aligned with the voice, although it cannot be determined exactly. All voices contain all elements. A metaphysically trained voice has the capacity of adapting itself to the purpose at hand. The voice becomes a tool to create resonance with one of the five elements.

Our thoughts and the source of our thoughts influence the quality of our vocal sound—the timbre and the rhythm. If we begin to open ourselves to our own innate higher energies, our voice color will go through changes. It acquires greater resonance, power, and spirit. We pull more energy through our subtle bodies and our true spiritual essence, linking them with our physical vehicle. By accessing our personal banks of spiritual energy, we alter the energy of our voices. The words and sounds we use gain strength and resonance, and they ring with an inner sense of authority.

The human voice conveys who you are through a unique combination of rhythm, melody, timbre and dynamics. It not only reveals who you are, but it also reveals from what sphere or plane you draw your greatest energy. Our voice is the personal vehicle for spiritual and creative expression. We do have a *voice image*, which pertains to the sound we produce and our persona. The voice image is the sound or the voice that we either like or dislike, identify with or refuse to identify with. It has nothing to do with vocal abilities, and it is formed predominantly by the culture around the individual (peer group, family, mass media, etc.). How to use the voice from a greater, more metaphysical realm is the key to discovering our true identity and the key to transmuting our energy and lives. We need to realize the full potential of our natural voice—that which we often fail to use.

Each voice represents a unique personality that defines an individual's character. Every voice has two predominant pitch levels: natural pitch level and habitual pitch level. If the two pitches differ, then the voice is being misused. This misused pitch may be too high or too low. We must learn to develop and enhance our natural voice frequency.

In Western society, people alter their natural pitch, creating an unnatural habitual voice. This is seen most often in business where a lowered, deepened voice conveys authority. Any pitch that is unnatural to the voice of the individual will strain the vocal mechanisms. We must learn to use our natural pitch and extend it, expand it to greater power and versatility. Unfortunately, today we adopt voices through imitation and without regard to our natural pitch frequency.

We must find the pitch and octave most comfortable for us. Such a voice should be projected from the "mask." The mask is the area from the nose bridge, the sides of the nose, down to and around the lips to the point where the jaw line links with the upper throat. A good exercise to determine whether or not you are projecting or speaking from the mask is to softly hum. Do the lips and the sides of the nose and chin vibrate? If so you are speaking from the mask. Or do you feel more of the vibration in the nose area or in the throat area? By learning to speak from the mask, the voice becomes more flexible and it is filled with greater expressiveness and warmth. It increases in its range and power, and its ability to resonate and create responses in others increases dramatically.

A basal voice (deeper tones) emanates from the lower part of the throat outside of the mask area. (There are deep voices which emanate from the mask which is ideal.) This basal voice is accepted and actually encouraged by our society, even if it is unnatural for most individuals. The high-pitched voice has been considered the bane of western society. This high pitch is created by constricting the lower throat when speaking as with a basal pitch, but the sounds are pushed higher. The nasal pitch is a third vocalization that is often unnatural, also frowned upon by society. It is the vocalization produced from the upper third of the vocal area or the nose area.

With the aid of a piano you can discover your natural pitch. In relation to middle C upon the piano, find the lowest and the highest note that you can sing without complete loss of quality. This is your singing range. In the average individual, it should be at least one and a half octaves, but whatever it is, we need to be aware of its range. The midpoint within that range corresponds most closely to your natural pitch. By working with it, through vocal exercises and especially by paying attention to speaking and singing from the mask, the voice becomes more flexible and the range increases. As the range increases, you have a greater ability to resonate with a wider spectrum of people and energies.

HIDDEN ASPECTS OF OUR VOICE

The sound created by an individual is a reflection of his or her general state of being and indicates the quality-of-life. This why many psychic and clairvoyants attune to the individual's voice for insight. The character of a person can be recognized within that voice if attuned to properly. A good experiment is to listen to the speech of another without listening to the words. Listen to the rate of speech, the volume, the pitches and the timbre of the voice itself. It takes some practice to do this without allowing the words to intrude, but learning to listen to the musical expression of the voice, the rate of speech and all other aspects will elicit great insight.

We all can distinguish the excessively nasal, breathy, or harsh voices. There are, however, many other subtleties. The voice can reveal suppressed anger and other emotional states. Our moods affect our voice quality. Tones and expressions that are short and staccato can indicate anger or nervousness. Prolonged tones are used by all of us when expressing love to someone. Our self-image also reflects itself within our voice. *Self-image* leads to *voice image* which reflects *self-image!*

The human voice is a wonderfully sensitive instrument. It has a profound influence upon the meaning and effect of our words. The language of our voices reflects our personalities. For example, people who are either very talkative or very taciturn usually have problems with their astral bodies as a result of emotional imbalances. A dull, uninteresting voice can indicate a depletion or lack of energy and vitality. In general, a higher pitched voice can reflect a mental orientation, while low sounds may imply physical inclinations. Nasal or uneven sounds normally indicate a blockage or imbalance within one of the chakras—usually throat or solar plexus. Off-pitch sounds usually indicate imbalance in one or more of the chakras. This in turn can reflect an individual's lack of perception concerning a troublesome aspect of his/her life. He or she is usually not acknowledging aspects of the self. These are, of course, generalities and must be applied in relation to the individual's natural pitch.

When adolescents go through puberty, their voices change. The cracking and changing voice indicates the opening and activation of the base chakra from a new level. It indicates the movement of the individual to develop and assert his or her own independent and individual energies.

Our emotions are closely related to the sound of our voice. The sound often reflects astral and mental body conditions, or emotional and mental states of being. Think of how many ways we could speak the following statement:

"I HAVE ALL I WANT."

It can be spoken with anger, pleasure, satisfaction, or hesitancy. What the sentence means will depend greatly upon how it is spoken by the individual, and every individual would probably express it differently.

Anger in a voice results in a higher pitch and a greater articulation of words (almost excessive articulation), with some syllables being intensely emphasized. Fear is reflected in a voice through sudden peaks, irregularities in pitch, and a faster, more precise articulation. People who habitually speak with these patterns may be reflecting fears on deeper levels. Perhaps they came into this incarnation in order to grapple with these fears. With sorrow or sadness, the articulation is slow. The vowels, consonants, and pauses are elongated. The voice trembles, and there are irregularities in voice quality—with usually a monotone at the end of the phrase.

The voice also reflects much of the evolutionary state of a person. The softness or loudness of the voice can show the natural condition of the individual at the time. Sometimes the spirit is tired, and sometimes the spirit may be strong. If the spirit of the individual is powerful, the voice will be powerful, and this is not reflected through volume. If the spirit of the individual loses vitality, the voice will also lose vitality. The light and darkness of the soul is revealed through the quality of one's voice. The voice responds instinctively to the energy and condition of the spirit and soul of the individual. It is for this reason that we need to increase awareness of the occult significance of speech.

THE HEALING ASPECTS OF VOICE

The voice has a tremendous ability to be an instrument for healing. Pythagoras recognized the considerable therapeutic power of human speech. He treated diseases through the reading of poetry. He taught his students how a skillful, well-modulated voice, with beautiful words and pleasing meter, could restore balance to the body and soul.

The belief in the healing capacity of the human voice is common to many parts of the world. Shamans and holy men of primitive societies would use a spirit language to commune with higher intelligences so as to extract proper remedies. The Huichal Indians believe that the soul or consciousness emits a high-frequency hissing or whistling noise. During times of illness, the soul strays from the physical body. The Huichal shamans mimic this sound in order to help attract the soul back to the physical body to restore health.

Confession has been used by many societies and religions as a means of accelerating the healing process. This process aligns itself with many of modern psychology's psychosomatic remedies. It was used voluntarily by the Apache Indians during times of illness. The Apaches recognized that all levels of consciousness and action were intimately connected to the physical. By confessing, the individual faced what had created the illness. The Eskimos would utilize a form of collective confession, believing that all illness was due to a violation of sacred taboos.

More commonly, the Catholic Church still utilizes confession. It has lost the physical healing aspects that once were associated with it. Today it is more focused upon the spiritual and emotional cleansing, and few today acknowledge its intimacy with physical well-being.

Our speech is comprised of two elements: consonants and vowels. The vowel sounds are the most dynamic aspect of spoken sound, for without them the consonants could not be sounded. Many of the early alphabets excluded the vowels, because they believed they were too stimulating, causing certain energies to be activated.

Every letter and combination of letters has significance. The Chaldean alphabet, one of the forerunners of our alphabet, was designed to be a tool for attaining higher wisdom. Their letters, sounds, glyphic forms, and their numerological correspondences provide clues to the more archetypal energies operating and activated through the words. We will explore a number of techniques in the next chapter describing how to employ these aspects in name magic and in the proper use of mystical words of power.

Mantra yoga is a technique of human self-realization through the use of inner sounds or nadas that are awakened through outer toning and chanting. In Tibetan beliefs, the most important musical instrument is the human voice, and the Tibetan shamans are trained in the use of outer sound projection to create inner, esoteric vibrations. They learn to use the head and chest as resonance chambers for the entire human body. The repeated toning of vowels creates a reverberation so that when the chanting stops, the sounds continue to echo within the mind and within the chambers of the body.

Each vowel opens a particular part of the body. This part of the body should be visualized during the inhalation and also when the vowel is spoken or toned internally. This inner sounding is the key to many metaphysical teachings concerning sound and mantras. Without the inner sounding occuring before the outer, audible sounding, the effects are minimized. The process of Directed Esoteric Toning involves both aspects. It is simple: as we inhale, we focus our minds on the region of the body associated with the vowel, and we sound it silently. Then as we exhale, we vibrate or tone the sound again audibly.

This method of opening by the vowels can be better understood if we realize that breath penetrates deeply into the region concerned, according to our thoughts. The breath takes the energy of prana and combines it with the vowel tones and together they open specific inner regions of the body or consciousness.

HEALING VOWEL SOUNDS

Vowel	Area of Body Opened by its Sounding
U	Pelvis, hips, legs, feet, and lower body in general.
O	Lower trunk, abdomen area from solar plexus to groin.
A	Chest cavity, heart, and the body as a whole.
E	Throat, upper chest, and head regions.
I	Back of the skull and head regions.

If with the aid of our thoughts and imagination we can suffuse our whole body with the vowel sounds, we can restore balance and life to all aspects of it. We can use the vowel sounds as an alternative to music in balancing and stimulating the chakras. Many people excuse themselves from the process of healing through sound, music, or voice by saying they can't play a musical instrument, they can't sing, they can't get to the library to borrow music in the appropriate key, they can't afford a five dollar pitch pipe, they don't know the song "Do, a deer..." or any number of reasons. If they have the capability of TELLING me why they can't employ music and sound techniques for healing, I've still got them. If they can speak, they can balance themselves.

In the previous chapter we discussed discussed musical tones, instruments, and vowel sounds that can be used to balance and stimulate chakra centers for physical and metaphysical purposes. Any short-circuiting within our energy system can be restored through the process of Directed Esoteric Toning with the vowel sounds, with mantras or with mystical words of power (as described in the next chapter). On the following page is a chart of vowels, their sounds, and their effects upon our energies.

TABLE OF CORRESPONDENCES
FOR QUICK REFERENCE

Vowel Glyph	Vowel Sounds	Chakras	Effects of Energy When Activated
A	ay (hay)	Heart	Chest, lungs, circulation, heart, blood. (Love, healing, balance, akashic memory).
	ah (cat)	Throat	Throat, respiration, mouth, trachea. (Creative expression, clairaudience).
	aw (saw)	Solar Plexus	Stomach, digestion, left-brain, intestines. (Inspiration, clairsentience, psychism).
I	I (eye)	Medulla Oblongata	Balanced brain function, mental clarity. (Mind over emotions, "intelligence of heart").
	Ih (bit)	Throat	Throat, respiration, mouth, trachea. (Creative expression, clairaudience).
E	ee (see)	Brow	Head cavity, sinuses, brain, pituitary, glands. (Clairvoyance, third eye, spiritual vision).
		Crown	Skeletal system, pineal. (Christ Consciousness).
	eh	Throat	Throat, respiration, mouth, trachea. (Creative expression, clairaudience).
O	oh (note)	Spleen	Muscular system, reproduction, navel area. (Creativity, reserve energy, higher emotions).
	aw (cot)	Solar Plexus	Stomach, digestion, left-brain, intestines. (Inspiration, power, psychic sensitivity).
U	oo (boot)	Base	Genitals, pelvis, lower body, circulation. (Vitality, life force, kundalini).
	uh (but)	Throat	Throat, respiration, mouth, trachea. (Creative expression, clairaudience).

DIRECTED ESOTERIC TONING

Toning is the process of vibrating sounds and tones (musical and spoken) to assist the healing process. It is cleansing, harmonizing and healing. It can be used to restore homeostasis to our energy system.

The voice releases power. It releases it in the direction of our thoughts, thereby sending the energy to the appropriate area of the body. We can use the sounds designed to balance the entire chakra system, or we can focus on the toning for just one particular area of the body.

1. Decide on the tone(s) to be used (the vowel sounds).

2. You may have the individual stand, sit, or lie down either facing toward you or from you. (Consult the last chapter of this book for a variety of healing techniques adaptable to the toning procedure.)

3. As you focus on the area to which you will project the tone, inhale slowly, sounding the tone silently in your own mind. Hold briefly, and exhale while audibly toning the sound. Project it out to the appropriate area of the person being balanced. If you are balancing yourself, simply focus your mind on that area, or fold both hands over it as you tone.

4. The sounds are toned in the manner best for you. There is no specific length of time to hold and project the tone, nor is there any specific volume. Allow the voice to find its own volume and pitch.

5. Remember to inhale, toning silently, and then exhale, toning audibly. Silent, audible. In, out. Spiritual, physical. We are activating the dynamics of sacred sound.

6. You may want to sing the tones in the appropriate note for the chakra. This can enhance the effects.

7. Pay attention to your own voice as you tone. Your voice will act like a sonar instrument, providing you with input. If your voice cracks and fluctuates as you tone, repeat the toning of that sound until the voice smooths itself out. This is an audible clue of balancing.

8. It is a good practice to tone the vowel sounds for each chakra, starting from the bottom, at least once a day. It does not take long, and it helps you to maintain your own balance. Do several repetitions of the sound for one chakra before moving on to the next.

9. In workshops, I demonstrate the effectiveness of toning the vowel sounds by finding someone who has back trouble or who cannot touch their toes when bending over. This is usually an indication of rigidity and blockage of the flow of energy through the spine. I perform the toning along their spine, as they stand in front of me, toning the vowel for each chakra 2-3 times. The process usually takes little more than a minute. I then have the individual bend over a second time, and the individual will be able to bend over much more easily, usually with a difference of several inches.

It could be said that the person bends more easily the second time because he or she has already stretched, from bending the first time. While this may be true in some cases, in chronic back problems a single, brief bending will make little or no difference. I have found that if I test someone at the beginning of the workshop, and then come back to them and perform the toning on them an hour later, the results will still be noticeable. I have found that it doesn't matter whether it is done immediately, an hour later or a day later. The first bending is simply to provide a parameter for comparison.

10. Repeat the toning process as needed. (In the chapter on "Techniques of Bardic Healing" there are several other toning techniques, including the use of toning in group healing situations.) Remember that as you balance another individual with the toning process, you are also balancing yourself.

Breath is important to the process of directed esoteric toning. Breath refers to that quick intake or gasp of energy that carries an image or thought to the subconscious. All aspects of toning are related to breath. Breath is life. When we become aware of our breathing patterns, we have greater control over them. As we work with toning and become more balanced, our breathing becomes more fluid, healthy, and harmonious.

The purpose of toning is to restore the vibrational pattern of the body (physical and subtle) to its perfect electro-magnetic field so that our spiritual essence can manifest more fully in our physical environment. Voice belongs to the physical body, but it is the instrument of the spiritual self. Being more than body, we need to learn to use it as a tool for higher consciousness and greater health. Experiment with the toning process. Take the primary vowel sound from your name. Close your eyes and tone the sound slowly. Allow it to find its own volume and length of sound. Initially, don't try and hold it to a particular pitch. Repeat for five to ten minutes. Within this time, it will find its own natural pitch. After a week of this, you will naturally tone the most harmonious pitch. This is effective in helping to develop greater resonance within your own voice. Toning this sound ten to twelve times is balancing to the body and calming to the mind.

Work with all of the vowel sounds. Start with the base chakra and tone each sound five to ten times, moving up through each chakra center. Use a pitch pipe and experiment with different pitches for the different vowel sounds. Pay attention to areas in which you have difficulty with the tone or at those points where the voice breaks, cracks or fluctuates.

The toning process can be used to heal yourself and to increase self-awareness. As with all healing, relaxation is critical, but the unique aspect of sacred sound is that relaxation occurs as a natural part of the process. You cannot use healing sounds without relieving stress.

Pay attention to yourself as you tone. Can you feel the sound in a particular part of the body? What is the effect? Is it comfortable? Agitating? energizing? Determine the feeling as best you can. Do not be discouraged if you can't label it. Toning is a learning process as much as it is a healing process.

As you notice the part of the body most strongly affected, think about the chakra associated with that part of the body. As you tone, visualize the chakra growing brighter, stronger and more balanced. What kind of energy does this stir? Is it calming? Firing? Does it draw you into harmony? Does it heal? As we begin to understand how the toning process affects you personally, you will have a better idea of how to apply it to others.

Experiment with the dynamics. Use different tones with different vowels. What happens when you soften the tones? What happens when you sing it louder? Play with the rhythms of it. Hold the tone for longer intervals and for shorter intervals. Pulse the tones. Mix the short and long tones.

Have fun with the process. As you play and experiment with it, you extend your normal range of voice, and you strengthen your resonance. You will find it easier to hold the tone. You will also find it is easier to speak in your natural pitch as opposed to your habitual vocal pitch.

THE THOUGHTFORMS OF SPEECH

In the physical world, we are known by our speech, our reticence, by the things we say or leave unsaid. We are judged by the quality of our conversation. In everyday activity, we all think and build speech. Much of it is not worthwhile, or it is vitalized with the wrong kind of energy. Speech is how we communicate while in the physical dimension. When we operate on other levels, our communication is less complicated. It operates along the lines of intuitive perception.

As we grow and our energy capacities are amplified, the thoughts are built stronger. They are vitalized by the spirit we are able to put into them. We can fill our words with greater energy. For this reason, any spoken word—if not based upon personality impulses—can create barriers of intense mental energy that can have repercussions.

Our thoughts affect the energy of our subtle and physical bodies. The stronger and more focused our thought processes, the stronger the effects. Thoughts mold the universal energy that surrounds us and is a part of us. The universal energy shapes the patterns within our energy field into forms and shapes that affect us on all levels. Part of working with the power of speech is understanding the concept of thoughtforms.

Thoughtforms are thoughts and ideas—energy patterns—which take on a particular form when given shape by our thinking. This can work to our benefit or detriment. Its strength is determined by the intensity of our thoughts and the length of time given to those thoughts. They are given added impulse through our words.

The quality, nature and definition of our thoughts determines the shape, clarity, and the color of our thoughtforms and of our auric field. The words we use to enhance or express our thoughts add to their intensity and strength. When a thought goes out toward an object, we are pouring out a subtle force. Our brain waves are electrical. The more we focus them, the stronger they become, altering the fabric of our auric field.

Every word we speak makes a thoughtform in the etheric and astral energy around us. Just as a thought creates a thoughtform upon the mental plane of existence, our words draw that energy out of the mental, crystallizing it into some manner of expression within the physical.

Some words take forms within the auric field, depending on their use. The word "hate" creates an ugly coloration within the auric field of the individual. This is partly due to its meaning, but also to the tremendous amount of energy given to it by so many people throughout the ages. It has a collective energy that is magnetically drawn to anyone using it.

Unpleasant words and their forms affect the atmosphere around the individual. This is why it is so difficult to be around someone who is extremely critical, pessimistic, or coarse. The individual who speaks in such a manner has developed a tolerance for or a resonance with those negative energy patterns. They don't understand why others avoid them. They don't understand that their thoughts and words have created an auric field that is discordant to others.

The aura can become permeated with negative energy patterns if exposed to them long enough. This is why those who are so often criticized become critical themselves. Our auric energy is an electro-magnetic field, constantly giving off and absorbing energy.

The energy forms of some words are not determined by the thought associated with the word. The thought builds its form of energy, but the word and its traditional use carries with it its own separate energy forms. This can create a combinations of contradictory energy patterns within the individual's auric field. For example, we have all used "hate" in ways that had no real emotion attached to it: "I hate brussels sprouts" or "I hate getting up early". In these cases, it doesn't hold any real emotion, but it can draw a thoughtform of energy associated with the use of that word to you.

Some words are problematic regardless of use—"hate" for example. Some are the exact opposite. Some create tremendous and beautiful thoughtforms and energy changes within the aura. "Love" is one such word. Understanding this helps us to understand the old aphorism, "If you can't say something nice, say nothing at all."

Part of the training in the ancient mystery schools required work in the control of speech, including regulating words and their meanings. The importance of accuracy and refinement in speech was strongly and strictly emphasized. Exaggerations are harmful. They irritate and aggravate the astral body. Contradictory phrases do likewise, i.e. "awfully good." It is because of contradictions in our speech that prayers and affirmations do not manifest the way we prefer.

Right speech and laughter have a beneficial effect upon all aspects of health and being. In the aura it can be seen as color. Being able to see the auric fields is an ability open to everyone, and not limited to clairvoyants. It is a matter of exercising and stimulating the cones and rods of the eyes to perceive more of the light spectrum, especially the subtle emanations around the body. With practice, the ability can be developed to see the effects of words upon those energy fields.

Unpleasant speech and laughter aggravates the energy and actually muddies up the auric field. The auric colors become darker, and often look smoky or cloudy. In extreme cases it appears as if a web of browns and grays is being formed around the physical body. This haziness hinders our health and blocks the flow of energy being mediated by the chakras. It muddies them up. This hinders the expression of our greatest abilities. It creates a form of "static electricity" around the physical body that must be loosened and cleaned out for health to be restored.

Control, discipline and awareness of speech is important. We must be cautious of casual or thoughtless remarks. The stronger and more developed we become, the greater the responsibility. Foolish things repeated time and again creates an atmosphere around us that can block the positive influences and energies. Off-color jokes and language produce forms that can cling to our aura and draw to us lower astral entities which stimulate even more of the same. And most important, we must remember that words spoken precisely and with meaning produce greater effects. And kind words and merriness never does harm!

NOTES TO CHAPTER THREE

1. Plutarch. "On Curiosity," *Moralia*. Sec. 519–c.

CHAPTER FOUR

Mystical Words of Power

Words, sound, and music can be applied to various aspects of our development. It does not require much work to be able to discern how effective they are in the healing realm, but they are also extremely powerful tools for heightened consciousness and perception. They can be used for inducing altered states of consciousness, facilitating astral projection, for trance, vision quests, and the awakening of creative faculties.

The ancient traditions were spiritual traditions aimed at altering, transforming, and expanding the human consciousness. This aspect can be assisted through ritual and ceremony. We can apply techniques of sacred sound in three specific areas to assist ourselves with this process: (1) the speaking of ritual words and sounds, (2) through the use of prayer and (3) through mantras and chants.

It is amazing how many people think along the lines of spells, incantations, and charms in association with anything metaphysical. Most of these opinions stem from the fabric of imagination—what has been displayed and distorted through T.V. and the movies over the past 25 years. Most of what has been seen, experienced and accepted by the general public is hype and reveals little understanding or knowledge of how sound and words align our energies with more dynamic and subtle dimensions.

Even today, with the prevalence of metaphysical knowledge, much information on ritual and the magical use of words and sounds is performed by the dabbler or psychic thrill-seeker who has little foundation. These individuals often invent practices to cover their own misbehavior, to proclaim themselves as something they are not, or for self-gratification.

It was once considered that rituals and the mystical use of words and sound concerned themselves only with demons and angels. What we must understand is that they can be used to harmonize body, mind and soul, thus aligning our physical selves with the more spiritual energies of life. A proper understanding of the use of mystical words of power assists us in this process.

SPEAKING RITUAL WORDS AND SOUNDS

The ancient god-names are specific signals, signals that can be used to call upon aspects of the one divine force throughout the universe. They are specific characteristics of the one divine force that is reflected in all powers. They represent particular manifestations of the divine within our universe.

It is said that to know someone's name is to have power over them. There is much truth and misconception in this. Unless we know the metaphysics and all of the correlations and significances of the name, we cannot truly have power over it or use it to the utmost.

The use of god-names in rituals, prayers, affirmations and mantras has been practiced probably as long as humanity has been upon the earth. They can be used to attune to the specific force represented by the name. It is the difference between using a generic title and a specific one. If we call out to a group of individuals, "Hey, you!," anyone may turn around. If we call out, "Hey, Joe!" Joe will be the one to turn around.

All names and words have their own magic if we learn how to use them. We must be careful, however, with our use of the ancient names and words of power. They will affect us differently because we live in a different environment. We respond to sounds differently, and we have greatly different energy systems. The words and names can still be effectively applied, but we must prepare and adjust those ancient energy patterns to the present. If we don't, they will evoke unbalanced responses within the individual.

It is amazing how frequently inquiries arise about specific words or phrases for different purposes, as if the words and phrases have been hidden away in some sacred vault. It is not the words that have been kept secret. These have been known since time immemorial. In fact, the most powerful name that a person can employ is his or her own. (Refer to the author's previous work on *The Sacred Power in Your Name* for further information on this.) The real mystery in using mystical words and names of power lies in the practiced discipline and usage of them.

The ancient names and words of power can open levels of consciousness that will facilitate manifesting the corresponding energies within our individual life circumstances. The use of the names over the centuries has established an automatic resonance between that aspect of the divine consciousness and the individual's. Its use links us to the thoughtform associated with it, which in turn establishes a bridge between us and the actual energies.

It is best and safest to practice with the more familiar words and names given in this chapter. It is also best to keep them in their archaic form or original language. This serves to prevent us from profaning them through misuse or ordinary conversation. It keeps an air of sacredness and power about them, so that when we do use them, they are even more significant. This is especially true of the more ancient names and words, as many of them go back to the earliest of times and thus have a capacity to touch primal cores of consciousness.

USING ANCIENT GOD-NAMES

1. Learn as much as you can about the name (or word) and its meanings before using it yourself. Try and learn how it has been used in the past, as this can assist you in understanding how its energies may manifest in your own life in the present. The more you understand its symbology, the more fully will it manifest.

2. Try and use the correct pronunciation. Remember that the sounds carry the impact and reflect quite a bit about the kind of energy responses we can expect from its use.

3. Tone the words and names, syllable by syllable, giving each equal emphasis. Hold the tone for as long as you feel comfortable.

4. Use the directed esoteric toning process with it. As you inhale, vibrate it silently, and then as you exhale, tone it audibly, syllable by syllable.

5. As you tone each syllable, keep in mind the significance of the name and the inner realities and energies with which it is associated.

6. Keep your tones smooth. Humming the names is very powerful. As you exhale, hum the name, vibrating it audibly and visualizing it traveling throughout your being and throughout the universe.

7. Utilize the practice of silent toning on the inhalation before vibrating the names audibly. Direct the inner tone to the inner world. The aim is to create a constant tone, moving from one dimension to the other. As you learn to work with the inner sound, you will develop the ability to hear the name echoed within your mind even while occupied at other tasks. This is a confirmation that you are building a bridge from the spiritual to the physical.

8. Sing the names and words in specific tones. Use your natural pitch or the tone you feel comfortable with. If you wish, you may use the god-names and tones from the Qabalistic Tree of Life, found on a chart in this chapter. This will amplify the effects.

9. Repeat for approximately ten minutes and then sit quietly, bringing your attention to what it is you desire from the energy released by the name. See it as if it is already yours. Visualize everything that could help in its manifestation.

10. Be cautious in using the ancient god-names, as they are powerfully effective—deceptively so. They can be like drawing from a divine energy-battery.

11. When awakening a divine aspect that lives within, we must aim the sound (by making ourselves very much aware of its concept) and then link it to ourselves through the vocalization. After awakening it, we direct it, so that it might become part of our faculties, wisdom, and understanding. Direct it toward a particular issue, problem, or area of enlightenment.

Do not generate energy just to generate energy. It needs to be grounded. Energy not directed will disrupt.

12. Each time that you use it, it will increase in its ability to work for you. Its energy will intensify in power and strength with repeated use and meditation. Remember that you are making these energy-batteries out of your own magical words.

We use the ancient divine names and words to invoke and awaken energies that are normally associated with them, yet that live within us. Even though the energies may be inherent, they must still be brought into manifestation. When we tone the names, we are aligning ourselves to that aspect of the divine creative intelligence represented by the name. When the sound of the divine name vibrates throughout our body and our consciousness, we bring our energy into resonance with it.

A good source for names are those which are aligned with any particular mythology to which you are drawn. Learn as much as you can about that mythology and the individuals represented within it. Learn to pronounce the names in the language of the mythology for even greater impact.

Another source for names is the ancient Hebrew Qabala. This system resonates strongly for any with a Judeo-Christian background. The ten god-names within the Tree of Life are ten manifestations of the divine within the physical world.

Regardless of the ancient tradition, the energies of the gods and goddesses with whom you work are all to be found within each of us without exception. When you use them, you and you alone will be their point of manifestation. All forms, images, and associated energies will come

GOD NAMES FROM THE QABALISTIC TREE OF LIFE

God Name & Tone	Energies Within Consciousness Affected by Names
EHEIEH (Eh Heh Yeh) Tone of B	Greater creativity; any final ending information; inner spiritual quest and its causes and attainment.
JAH / JEHOVAH (Yah Ho Vah) Tone of A#	Greater personal initiative; a source of energy which puts things in motion; Father-type information; realization of one's abilities.
JEHOVAH ELOHIM (Yah Ho Vah-Eh Lo Heem) Tone of A	Greater understanding of sorrows and burdens; Mother-type information; understanding on its deepest level; for strength through silence; understanding anything secretive.
El (Ehl) Tone of G	Greater sense of obedience to the Higher; financial gains, opportunities; building the new; justice; abundance; prosperity; hearing the inner call.
ELOHIM GEBOR (Eh lo Heem Guh Bor) Tone of F#	Greater energy and courage; for tearing down of old forms; for change of any kind; critical judgement; information on enemies & discord.
JEHOVAH ALOAH vaDAATH (Yah Ho Voh Ay Lo Ah Vuh Dahth) Tone of F	Greater and higher sense of devotion; all matters of healing, life and success; for harmony on any level and any matter; awakening of Christ consciousness; glory and fame.
JEHOVAH TZABAOTH (Yah Ho Voh Zah Bah Oath) Tone Of E	Greater unselfishness; understanding and power in relationships; sexuality and elements of nature; creativity and the arts; love and idealism.
ELOHIM TZABAOTH (Eh Loh Heem Zah Bah Oath) Tone of D	Greater truthfulness; revealing of falsehood & deception around us; greater ability in communications, learning, magic, wheelings and dealings.
SHADDAI EL CHAI (Shah Dy Ehl Hy) Tone of Middle C	Greater sense of true independence and confidence; greater intuition and psychic ability; mental and emotional health; dream work; understanding and recognition of the tides of change.
ADONAI HAARETZ (Ah Doh Ny Hah Ah Ratz) Tone Of F	Greater ability to discriminate in your life; to overcome a sense of inertia in life; physical health problems of self and others; affairs of home; greater self-discovery; elemental life.

through you and into your life. What you are inside will color how the energies manifest outside. You are the channel, and you must learn to discern their effects in your life as you use them.

The following three names are effective to experiment with to begin to understand the power of mystical words:

Amen

In the Hebrew tradition, this word translates as "so be it" or "it is truly," but when used as a god-name, it is tied to the Egyptian tradition and takes on a different correspondence. This is the name for the primal parent, the cosmic element which first created life within the chaos of the universe.

It has ties to the great being of Egyptian tradition, Amen-Ra. It is a divine name. It represents the divine producer of life. Although often depicted as a male figure, it embodies the true essence of the male and female, the father and the mother. Whenever the male and female come together, birth occurs. As an invocation or even within a prayer, it is a call to that aspect of the one divine force that gives life to our prayers. It is an affirmation that the father and mother principles operate within the universe and within ourselves and can give birth to the fulfillment of our prayers. It is the father/mother expressing and living within the child, giving to all children the ability to create and give birth as well. When sung, the two syllables should be sung to the tones of F-sharp and G—symbolic of the raising of energy to a higher vibration and the assertion of the will force in the manifestation process. (G is the tone for the throat chakra, the center for higher creativity and will.)

Hu (Hoo)

Simply translated, this ancient Sufi word means "He." It is the name for the father-god aspect living within all of humanity. *HU*man is the god in man and woman.

Eheieh (Eh-Heh-Yeh)

This name for the divine, drawn from the Hebrew Qabala, translates as "I am that I am." It is the name for the life breath manifesting in all living things. It is the divine, white brilliance existing within the consciousness of humanity. It is the link to our most spiritual level of consciousness manifesting through the physical body and the world.

In many rituals, aspects of the divine were associated with each of the four directions of the world. These were usually sectioned off within the temple itself. The divine names or mystic words were sung in harmonics, creating a chord effect, invoking the energy of the divine on all levels. When sounded or sung together, it raised the energy of the entire temple and created a powerful resonance among the participants of the ritual and the divine force being invoked.

For example, if we were to use the name "EHEIEH" to raise an awareness of the "I AM" aspect of the temple, the participants would be divided into four sections. These four sections are symbolic of the four directions of the world. One tone would be assigned to the Eastern Quarter as the keynote. (The sun rises in the East.) The other directions would then sing the name in harmonic intervals of that keynote:

EAST: Middle C.

WEST: G above middle C (the dominant or fifth in the harmonic interval).

SOUTH: E or E-flat (The third in the harmonic interval; the flat is considered more natural).

NORTH: B-flat (The seventh in the harmonic interval).

In this example we have created a C7 chord, so that when the name is sung, a tremendous generator of energy is established within the temple. This brings the sound full circle, back to the east and on a higher octave. This enables prayers or other ritual purposes to extend more strongly and stimulate greater response in the participants. You can also do this by yourself. Sing each of the harmonics of the directions yourself in the order given (East, West, South, and North).

THE POWER OF PRAYERS

In prayers are expressed the more commonly known aspects of the power of the Word. Prayer has long been a vital part of all religious teachings. Prayer plays an important part in our destinies.

It is the destiny of modern man and woman to conquer matter. The quest for our innermost self is a path that enables us to bring out our spiritual essence to play upon the plane of matter. This is why we have so many churches. They assist us in this, but unfortunately, their true purposes are often misunderstood. They end up promoting theological doctrines rather than spiritual perceptions.

Theology is humanity's attempt to understand the divine. It is not the divine's commentary upon our individual lives. In and of itself, it holds little importance to a true spiritual life, for the only thing that truly matters is the desire of the soul for the divine. If the desire is there, the soul will find its path.

TABLE OF CORRESPONDENCES

Chakra	Tone	Sound	Mantram	Color	Attribute	Healing Property
ROOT	Middle C (Do)	ŭ (ooo)	Lam	Red	Vitality, kundalini, life force.	Circulation, low blood pressure, colds and shock.
SPLEEN	D (Re)	ō (oh)	Vam	Orange	Creativity, reserve energy, sexual.	Muscles, reproduction, detoxifying, emotional balance, sexuality.
SOLAR PLEXUS	E (Mi)	aw / ah	Ram	Yellow	Inspiration, intellect, wisdom, psychism.	Digestion, laxative / constipation, headaches, adrenals.
HEART	F (Fa)	ā (ay)	Yam	Green	Love/healing, balance, Akashic memory.	Heart trouble, lungs, ulcers, hyper-tension, blood/circulation.
THROAT	G (Sol)	ĕ (eh) ŭ (a / uh)	Ham	Blue	Clairaudience, cooling, relaxing.	Throat, fevers, asthma, lungs, thyroid, antiseptic stimulation.
BROW	A (La)	ĭ / ē (ih / ee)	Aum/Om	Indigo	Third eye, clairvoyance spirituality.	Purifier (blood), obsessions, coagulant, sinuses, headaches,, stroke afflictions.
CROWN	B (Ti)	e (ee)	Om	Violet	Christ consciousness, inspiration.	Soothing to nerves, stress, confusion, neurosis, insomnia, skeletal problems.
SOUL STAR (trans-personal / 8th chakra	HIGH C (above middle C)		Om	Purple or Magenta	That part of soul linked to matter; link to our true spiritual essence.	Building the Body of Light, key to burning away negative thoughtforms that hinder physical and spiritual health for discipleship.

All churches, all religions, all mystery systems and all metaphysical philosophies are nothing more than props to support and steady the mind and consciousness while it prepares itself. Their purposes should be to help lead the consciousness through various stages of realization—to open it more, to expand its awareness, its reach and its application to our individual lives. To assist us in this is the power of prayer.

The ancient masters used prayer as a powerful technique for implanting positive suggestions—particularly in the healing process. They would scan the individual and view the conditions of the physical and subtle bodies. They would perceive the deep-seated illusions and energy patterns, and through a strongly-voiced prayer or suggestion, they restored balance to the individual. They employed, through the power of the word, a forced resonance with the individual.

The process used involves two steps. After the scanning, a health-giving thoughtform is constructed within the mind, one with great intensity. Through the prayer and words, that thoughtform is projected out to impact the energy system of the individual. The use of visualization, will, and verbal projection transmutes the old condition, creating a new one in its place. (This is the true essence of prayer, reflected in Biblical scripture with the use of the phrase "You are healed.")

Our concepts of prayer and its proper usage has become distorted. Our prayers have become rote recitations or simple wish-making. Prayer is a process of concentrated visualization, combined with emotional and mental energizing, and then a grounding of these into the physical through proper vocalization. It should lead to achieving union of body, mind, and soul because it involves the energies of all. Prayer and sacred sound are direct links between humanity and the divine, but unless our words and sounds have meaning, they never get past the etheric webs of doubt and negative energies that we have formed about us.

We use affirmations and prayers, and even when they are fulfilled, the first thing most often said is, "The most amazing thing just happened!" The truly amazing thing would be if our prayers were not answered. They are supposed to be.

Proper use of prayer helps us to stretch ourselves. If utilized and vocalized with proper visualization, every thought, wish, desire, and aspiration can become an act of prayer. We can set energy in motion for their manifestation. It operates according to the Law of Cause and Effect. What we put out, we get back.

Prayer is dialogue that institutes change. It is a dialogue with the universe and with the divine. Most importantly, it is dialogue with those parts of yourself that resonate with the divine. It is dialogue with that part of your being that has the ability to create any condition you need or desire. It operates for all of us, but only according to our level of energy and consciousness. The more we realize that the divine lives within us, the more we are able to create through the power of prayer.

The invocation within prayer unites our meditative state of consciousness with the power of the Word and with our innate force of will. It takes practice to construct the proper formula for fulfillment of prayers, and each of us must find the formula that works best for us. There are, of course, guidelines.

Once you find the formula and begin to change and grow, so will your formula for prayer. When used properly, it will lift the veils. This is why affirmations are important. They start the process of creating the appropriate atmosphere and energy change within the aura. They help clear the webs so that the energy of our prayers can issue forth more productively.

It has been said, "Ask and it shall be given," but we have to learn how to ask. There are basics to the prayerful asking:

1. Proper visualization (concentrated and specific) of that for which you are praying. You must see it as if it is already yours.

2. There must also be an emotional energy applied to the prayer. This is not the emotion of desiring, but rather it is the emotion of anticipating. Anticipate the answer to your prayer as if you have picked it out of a catalogue and are simply waiting for UPS to deliver it to your door.

3. There must be a vocalizing of it in a specific, confident manner. This vocalization is more effective if you:

    *   include a reference to some divine aspect operating within the universe and within you.

    *   include an affirmation of you being a part of that divine aspect.

    *   allow the universe to bring it to you in the time, manner and means that is best for you.

    *   allow it to be invoked into your life for the good of all and according to the free will of all.

4. Pay close attention to the Law of Receiving once you start using your prayers. Often as we pray for something big, within several days little things may come into our life as well. Someone may pay you a compliment or offer you their assistance. Do not shrug those little things off. If we refuse to receive the little things the universe will not send us the big things. Often it is

the little things that start the magnetic pull and are the precursor of the manifestation of the big things.

Our doubts and fears delay answers to our prayers. They set up blocks and hindrances. Once set in motion, the energy of our prayers must play themselves out, but they must be allowed to do so in the time that is best for us. Do what you have to do and then let it take its own course in the fulfillment.

Any inaccuracy in your prayers may bring results you cannot use or do not need. Keep your prayers (especially personal prayers) secret! Not silent, but secret. This prevents their energies from being interfered with by others. It prevents others from sowing seeds of doubt as to the validity of your prayers. How often have you started a project and told your friends about it, only to have them relate how difficult it will be or what catastrophe happened when their uncle, aunt, brother, cousin, or, friend attempted it. There is strength in silence. With personal prayer, reticence is important to success.

MANTRAS AND CHANTS

Mantras comprise the seventh school of yoga. The word itself is Sanskrit, and it is comparable in meaning to our English words of "charm" or "spell." With mantras, the power of sound is used to convey an overriding spiritual reality to our consciousness.

Mantras can be used for various effects. They have a creative power and they can attract specific situations and conditions as they dynamically change the auric field of the individual. They also can have a destructive power that can be used to shatter or repel negative energies. They have the power to synthesize our energies, bringing har-

mony on all levels of our being. In tantra, there are ten kar-
mas of mantras (ten uses):

1. Healing.

2. Paralyzing (ability to stop the movement of any
   living thing).

3. Attracting (on any level).

4. Unbalancing (to disrupt or disturb equilibrium).

5. Controlling.

6. Distant attraction.

7. Change (to alter behavior).

8. Opposition (the creation of).

9. Death.

10. Increase and expansion.

Mantra yoga utilizes words, phrases and/or sounds
which carry power to effect changes in the mind, body,
emotions, or spirit of the individual. It stimulates the energies in the space outside and inside us, bringing both into
harmony and resonance with each other. Mantras have
the capacity to destroy hindrances to growth, and legends
tell us they could even be used to re-generate organs.

Many mantras, unless properly intoned, have no effect. When seen or heard by the uninitiated, it may appear
meaningless. To be able to correctly pronunce the mantra
of a deity often depends upon bodily and spiritual purity,
as well as the knowledge of proper intonation.

It is often believed that the psychic energy awakened
by some mantras can become poisonous on some level, if
it is awakened in a polluted sphere. Thus, as we grow and
raise our individual vibrations and become more spiritual, the mantras themselves take on even greater power.
It is important to treat them with respect.

The vibration of the mantram will set up a purifying and refining effect upon ourselves and our auric field. It will create opportunities to expel from our energy field coarser elements and energies. Indian and Mahayana Buddhist mantras are used to focus the mind, as the essence of many mantras is monotony. It's repeated so that the reality of the sound becomes dominant, and the mind wanders less within the meditative process.

Mantras work on any one of four levels (or their combinations). First, they work simply because of our faith that they will. Second, they work because we associate definite ideas with the sounds, which then intensifies the changing of our thoughts and feelings. Third, they work because of what they mean. The meaning beats itself into our mental body, which results in an impression being formulated within the energy pattern of the individual. Fourth, they work by their sound alone—without reference to their meanings. The sound vibrations create changes. The changes affect the function of the chakra system, thereby affecting the entire energy system.

There are seven seed sounds of the Sanskrit language. These seven mantras can be used to activate and balance the chakra centers in the same way that musical notes and vowels do. Included in this chapter is a chart that delineates all three aspects—musical notes, vowel sounds and mantras—in relation to the chakra system.

Most often the mantras are chanted. Chanting is a process that releases energy. It makes the recital of mystical words and sounds both mysterious and private. The rhythm of the chanting is critical, as it determines the hypnagogic or altered state of consciousness to be achieved. Fast chanting exhausts the breath and mind, but it is always followed by a dynamic state of relaxation. Slow chanting relaxes the breath and mind while the chanting is being done. This is most effective when done alone. A medium rate of chant is best in group situations. The medium rate does not disturb the rhythms of the breath, heart, and mind. It serves to make one more alert and vibrant.

Much of the science of chanting has been lost. It can evoke very fiery energies, but the energy is created according to the level of focus, concentration, and consciousness of the individual. Chanting must be controlled, as it will affect your life as well as the lives of those you touch, because it triggers a powerful reverberation of overtones.

Mantras and chants that depend upon the power of sound are most effective in the language in which they originated. A good mantram or chant will harmonize the body on all levels. It usually will consist of a predominance of long, open vowels, and it is designed to impose a new rate of vibration upon you—a forced resonance.

Chanted mantras have dynamic effects. Some sources say it is best to chant a mantram 1000 times. Others say less. As in all things, you must decide what works best for you. Ten to fifteen minutes is a very effective period to instill and awaken the vibration and feel its effects.

Chants and mantras are labor-saving devices in our development. They help us to focus the mind. We can learn to do it through strength of will, but mantras and chants make it easier and are quite enjoyable as well.

The power of mantras can intensify the effects of your own energy field. They can amplify negativity just as easily as they can intensify creativity. If they create headaches or feelings of faintness, you should stop. Certain angels, devas, and divine forces and beings are associated with many mantras. When you use the words and sounds, you are inviting their energies into your life. If your own consciousness and energy is not capable of handling their higher vibrations, the result may be imbalance and disharmony. Remember there is no quick and easy way to development. Moderation is the key—especially when treading in new areas.

The process of working with chants or mantras is simple. Choose a mantram, familiarize yourself with any significance or meaning that it might have. Choose a time in which you will not be disturbed and allow yourself to relax. Begin chanting the mantram, syllable by syllable. Allow it to find its own rhythm and volume, one that you are comfortable with. Continue this for ten to fifteen minutes.

As you stop, you will continue to hear the mantram echoing within your mind. There may even be a slight buzzing in the ears. These are clues that it has activated energy and brought it into the physical dimension. Sit quietly and meditate upon the energies. See them active within your auric field. Contemplate how you will use these new energies in your outer life.

During this meditative stage, make self-observations. Do you see any colors in your mind's eye? If not, what color would you imagine to be strongest around you at the moment? What color are you more drawn to at this time? See the color. Visualize it and feel it suffusing your entire being. Are there any other feelings or impressions that you are experiencing?

Focus on how much more light and energy has been awakened within you. Imagine and visualize how much more you will be able to accomplish with all of this new energy. See this energy radiating out and around you, touching and brightening all within your life.

SAMPLE MANTRAS

Om

The Om is considered the most powerful mantram of all. It corresponds to the Egyptian "AMEN" and actually represents the name of the Divine Logos. The Om is the Lost Word. It is the spark of life within the self, that part of the divine imprisoned within the physical dimension. We are here to find our release. We are here to find that Lost Word of our own.

There are several hundred ways of pronouncing and intoning the Om—each with its own unique effect. When we emphasize and prolong the "O," we affect one another and the energy of the auric field. When the "M" (the humming sound) is prolonged, the entire effect is produced internally, awakening the divine within us.

When we sound the Om, we need to see ourselves rising from the domination of physical life. We need to visualize our limiting and hindering thoughtforms being shattered. The Om is the sound of contact with the divine, and thus it is an instrument of our release. It has the power to release and create anew so that we can move on to higher realms and realizations. As we work with it, the tone will change, an audible clue that we are moving forward.

The Om is also a call to attention. It arranges the particles of our subtle bodies into alignment. Every particle of energy within us responds to the sound of Om. When our energies are in alignment, we are in the best possible position to benefit from our meditations and prayers. This is why it is often used as a prelude to meditations and prayer.

The Om is also a call to other beings of light. It lets them know that you are bringing your energies into alignment and balance, and thus it serves to enable them to draw closer to you.

A variation of this is AUM. Instead of the two sounds of O and M, there are now three—"Ah-Oh-mm." This form enhances visualization, so that thoughts can become more crystallized. It attracts energies from the subtler planes surrounding us so that we can more easily build our thoughts into reality. It is an affirmation that they will come into existence—"So Let It Be!" The Aum helps us to repair and rebuild while the Om helps us to release and harmonize.

The Om is a symbol of the path of return. It is used in meditation for release and resurrection. Simply relax, and choose a tone or note that is good for you. Inhale, sounding the Om silently. Exhale and sound the Om audibly. Do not rush, and allow the Om to find its own rhythm. Make sure you employ two sounds, the sound of the O and the M.

Om Mani Padme Hum
(Ohm-Mah-Nee-Pad-May-Hum)

This mantram translates as "the jewel in the lotus." It is one of the more popular mantras, and it has a variety of meanings and significances. It is believed to be a link to the Great White Brotherhood and particularly to the Goddess Kwan Yin.

Kwan Yin is to the East what the Mother Mary is to the West. She is the protector and healer of children. Legend states that as she achieved enlightenment and began to ascend from the earth plane, she heard the cry of a human and chose to stay behind and assist humanity. She is the Chinese goddess of mercy and children. She has the ability to negate any act of violence directed at anyone. Legends also state that her energy is so strong and pure that she can walk through 1000 legions of demons and devils and never be harmed or swayed from her destination. This mantram is considered by many as a direct call to her for protection.

The six syllables of this mantram reflect aligning oneself with a path of wisdom that can transform the impure body, speech, mind, doubts and fears into pure energy and consciousness of an enlightened master. Its energies are helpful in finding the balanced expression of spiritual method and wisdom for your own life circumstances.

Om:

This is the totality of sound and existence. It is the calling signal. By resonating this, you can set up a link to Kwan Yin and bring energies into alignment so that the path best for you to achieve the Buddhic state can be seen.

Mani:

This literally means "jewel." It refers to a kind of non-substance that is impervious to harm or change. It is a symbol of the highest value within the mind. It symbolizes enlightenment with compassion and love. Just as a jewel can remove poverty, so can an enlightened mind remove difficulty in a cyclic physical life experience. It has a vibration that awakens the energy for the fulfillment of human wishes.

Padme:

This means "lotus." It is the symbol of spiritual unfoldment where the jewel or Mani is obtained. It is the link to the crown chakra. If it is opened, unfoldment of our creativity occurs more quickly and positively. It has a sound that awakens wisdom from the muddied experiences of our life. This kind of wisdom assists us in not being contradictory.

Hum:

This sound is untranslatable, per se. While the Om represents the infinite sound within us and the universe, the Hum represents the finite within the infinite. It stands for potential enlightenment. It indicates indivisibility. Purity must be achieved by a unity of method and wisdom within one's own unique life circumstances. Om and Hum are more than just syllables. Properly used, they have the power to awaken within us higher states of consciousness and an intuitive understanding of truths that are difficult to clothe in words themselves.

THE ASTROLOGICAL OM

Another powerful way of using the mantram Om is in conjunction with the musical tones associated with the astrological chart. This particular method corresponds to forms of transcendental meditation. In transcendental meditation, the individual is given a three syllable mantram that is his or hers alone.

In astrology, three predominant parts of our astrological chart are linked to the signs in which the sun, the moon, and the ascendant were located at the time of birth. They reflect a major aspect of our inherent energy potentials. Determine the notes for each of these aspects in your own astrological chart, using the charts found in Chapter Two "Music of the Spheres." For example, using the second diagram on the page, if your Sun was in Cancer, your Moon in Taurus and Aquarius was your ascendant, your three predominant tones would be G-sharp, F-sharp and A.

Using a simple pitch pipe, we can sound each tone and then vibrate the mantram Om to each of those notes. After several minutes, you won't need the pitch pipe. You will be able to sing the Om in the notes most appropriate for these astrological aspects. This is extremely balancing to the physical, emotional, mental, and spiritual energies of the individual. Sing or vibrate the Om as long as you wish.

Altering the order of the tones has its unique effects as well. You can develop variations to bring out specific energies and elicit specific effects. You have, in essence, created your own unique transcendental mantram.

PART TWO

The Renaissance of the Bardic Traditions

Whenever misfortune threatened the village, the Rabbi would retreat to a special place in the forest, light a sacred fire and say a special prayer. The misfortune was then avoided. As time passed, this task fell to another Rabbi who know the special place in the forest and the special prayer, but he did not know how to light the sacred fire. Still misfortune was avoided. Finally the task fell to yet another Rabbi over the years who knew neither the place in the forest, how to light the sacred fire or even the special prayer. All he could do was tell the story to others, but that was sufficient![1]

—A variation on an old Hassidic tale

CHAPTER FIVE

A History of the Mystical Bards

In every society, in every part of the world, there were individuals whose task it was to keep the ancient mysteries alive and to pass them on by word of mouth. These individuals were historians, musicians, and healers. They are what we now group under the generic term of "bard."

Through myths, tales, parables, poetry, and song they kept their traditions and their esoteric mysteries alive for their peoples. The African griots, the Norse skalds, the Anglo-Saxon gleemen, the French troubadours, the Navajo singers, the Russian kaleki, the Indian magahda and the Japanese zenza are all part of this ancient bardic tradition. They were all healers, entertainers, and teachers.

The bards were commonly believed to be mere entertainers, but the earliest of their traditions involved great training in all aspects of physical and metaphysical phenomena. It is generally accepted that the bards as entertainers evolved from the tradition of the wandering shaman—who was healer, clairvoyant, and singer in one.

Song and sorcery often went hand in hand in the earliest of the bardic traditions. The Norse figure of Odin was not only the master of mystic laws but also of poetry. In the sixth century of Greece, strolling minstrels doubled as fortune tellers. And even more familiar to us in modern times are the traditions of the gypsy minstrels and fortune tellers.

The true mystic bard would use the allegory of story and myth to present truths to the society in the manner which the society could accept them. It is often difficult to distinguish the religious and mystical storytelling from that which was mere entertainment, as both aspects were often blended together so that each listener could respond and receive at his or her own level.

Storytelling was a means of passing on teachings without profaning them. The earliest of the storytellers would infuse their myths and tales with images and allegories that would resonate with the hearts and minds of their people. The true mystic bard knew how to choose a story and images appropriate to his or her audience. Eventually, the sacred teachings came to be jealously guarded and the bards evolved into mere entertainers, historians, and praise singers.

There came to be many ranks of bards, the lowest of which was termed the "bard." Those that were more schooled and professional would use other names and titles. They were often distinguished not only by their skill in music and song, but by the instrument that they used. The Greek rhapsodists were distinguished from the amateur Greek bard by the fact that they could perform on the kithara, while the amateurs performed on the lyre alone.[2] The Ollahms of the Irish Bardic tradition were considered more in the lines of the poet laureate, while the Shanachies were more historical in their narratives. The Magadha of

India was the best of the Indian minstrels, and this title later became a name for the great center of Buddhism.

It is often difficult to distinguish the bard from the storytelling process. Which came first? "The question has often been asked: did these bards, minstrels, rhapsodists and the like precede or follow the telling of tales by persons not looked upon as professionals? Did this special career develop as a secularization of original priestly or religious functions? Or were the first storytellers merely the best from among those who entertained their particular social group informally, then realized their special talents and power, and gradually sought to protect their status by devising systems regulating training, practice and performance?"[3]

Regardless, it is evident that the two cannot be separated. We cannot examine the bardic tradition without also examining the important role of storytelling and myths in the esoteric traditions. Myths and tales are of great importance in many societies —especially to the development of the people within those societies.

Bardic activity is depicted in Egyptian art and hieroglyphics. Biblical scripture is filled with folklore about individuals teaching through tales. Sanskrit literature contains passages that reflect storytelling for both religious and secular purposes. There are references in the *Upanishads* and Vedic literature. The Buddhist *Tipitaka*, its sacred scripture, contains tales of many types. Taoism used stories to spread and reinforce its beliefs. The writings of Chang Tze includes parables and short stories of Confucius, Lao Tze and other heroes. In the Hindu religion, the *Brahmanas* contain myths and stories to explain the Vedas. The ancient Hasidic-Judaic tradition considered storytelling as the best way to introduce religious beliefs and their practice. They often used classic fables or popular anecdotes and then attached a moral.

There are many historical references to the bardic process of storytelling. Legends of Cassiopeia date to 3500 B.C. The Chinese tales of the Pleiades date to around the year 2000 B.C. Homer wrote *The Illiad* and *The Odyssey* between 950 and 850 B.C. *The Elder Edda* of the Teutonic tradition dates to only 800 years ago. An old Finnish tale composed over 3000 years ago, *The Kalevala* includes a description of the Finnish sagaman:

> I am wanting, I am thinking
> to arise and go forth singing,
> Sing my songs and say my sayings,
> Hymns ancestral harmonizing,
> Lore of kindred lyricking.
> In my mouth the words are melting;
> Utterances overflowing
> to my tongue are hurrying . . .
> So that we may sing good songs,
> Voice the best of all our legends
> For the hearing of our loved ones,
> Those who want to hear them from us . . .
> Magic verses we have gathered,
> Kindled by the inspiration . . .
> Magic never failed the Sampo,
> Louhi never lacked for spells . . .
> There are other words of magic,
> Incantations I have learned,
> Plucked in passing from the wayside . . .
> Then the frost was singing verses,
> Many a rhyme the rain recited,
> Other poems the wind delivered,
> On the seawaves songs came drifting,
> Magic charms the birds have added
> And the treetops incantations.[4]

Through the Greek civilization we have many historical references to the bards and rhapsodists and the storytelling process:

- Homer in *The Odyssey*.[5]

- Plato's *Republic*.[6]

- Ovid in *Metamorphoses*.[7]

- Aristotle in *Politics*[8] (along with the entire work of *Rhetoric*).

- Cicero in *De Oratore*.[9]

Throughout the Middle Ages, the bardic tradition gradually lost its mystery—and its strong connections to the esoteric arts. The healing and enlightening aspects gave way to the entertaining, however, they were still in demand. The bards ranged in social status, but regardless of their individual status, itinerant musicians and storytellers were seen in every part of Europe.

In the beginning, they were an accepted part of both secular and religious activities. Song and dance were fundamental to medieval life, even in the Church. Singing and dancing in the Church took forms of ritual which were adapted from ancient traditions. Celebrations were staged to coincide with midwinter, midsummer and the equinoxes. Throughout the Middle Ages, the lines between secular and church affairs was still malleable.

Then the Church began to warn against the traveling musicians because of the ties between the songs and stories they used and the ancient mystical traditions. The Council of Tours in 813 warned priests to avoid "immodesties of dishonest actors and their obscene amusements." The Bishop of Orleans soon after banned singing of "rustic poems" and indecent performances by female dancers.

The Council of Avignon declared in 1209: "We have decreed that at the vigils of the saints (held on the eve of major religious festivals) there should not be in the churches any of this theatrical dancing, these immodest rejoicings, these meetings of singers with their worldly songs which incite the souls of those who hear them to sin."

The troubadours of France were pre-eminent among the singer-poets of medieval Europe. They were comprised of men and women, and through their poetry they sought to elevate the Lady and thus the ancient concept of Sophia of medieval gnosticism—the divine feminine wisdom. But by the 1300's, the activities and acceptance of the troubadours, minstrels, and bards had faded tremendously.

The bardic tradition, although faded, is not lost. The stories and myths still live, and the great archetypal energies and esoteric teachings can still be extracted from them. In the Western world, we have lost touch with our myths, and so we must learn to re-connect. We must again dig into the roots of our civilization and re-create our folklore. Joseph Campbell wrote, "There is a romantic idea that myth comes from the people. It doesn't; it comes from the teacher, the shaman, and visionary as the giver and interpreter of myth." [10] This was the goal and the task of the ancient bardic students—to breathe new life and power into the words and images of our tales and myths. This must become the task of the modern bard as well.

"Children play at being great and wonderful people, at the ambitions they will put away for one reason or another before they grow into ordinary men and women. Mankind as a whole had a like dream once: everybody and nobody built up that dream bit by bit, and the ancient storytellers are there to make us remember what mankind would have been like, had not the fear and the failing will and the laws of nature tripped up its heels . . . I have read in a fabulous book that Adam had but to imagine a bird and it was born into life, and that he created all things out of himself by nothing more than unflagging fancy; and heroes who can make a ship out of a shaving have but little less of the divine prerogatives."

—William Butler Yeats
in his preface to Lady Gregory's
Gods and Fighting Men.

BARDIC TRAINING

Each mystery tradition had its own keynote or key theme. It was important for the student bard to dig into the roots of his or her civilization and discover the esotericism of its folklore. Those who wish to resurrect this process must do likewise. Look to the origins of the ancient myths, and look at their similarities. What is the origin and significance of the Arthurian legends, the Nibelungenlied, the Volksunga Saga, the Ossianic Cycle, Beowolf, Robin Hood, Hiawatha, Coyote Trickster, the Bushmen Mantis tales? We've lost touch with our myths, and we must learn to create them anew in the tradition of the ancient bards.

An Ethiopian proverb states, "When the heart overflows, it comes out through the mouth." This is appropriate to the ancient art of and training in the bardic tradition. As the individual was awakened to the dynamic energies of the universe, these would be relayed to others through the dynamics of storytelling.

There are legends and tales about many of the ancient schools of wisdom that dealt with the power of the Word. The Schools of Prophets in Biblical scripture was founded by Samuel who was the great initiate-singer of his day. Song and dance was the way to liberate the soul from the body and connect to the Divine Feminine Wisdom of the universe. The next of the great initiate singers of the school of prophets was David, who used his harp as a symbol. Many of the Biblical psalms are attributed to him and cannot fully be experienced unless sung. Elisha (the prototype of Jesus) used the harp to induce a prophetic state.

In Arabia, training was given in the writing of Islamic poetry to lift the soul to ecstasy. In the Norse lands, scaldcraft was the primary teaching of the inner schools of music. And the Irish spent years of training: "The Irish poet-tellers studied their art for 15 years and had to be wise in philosophy, astronomy, and magic and conversant with 250 prime tales and a hundred subsidiary ones. The shanachies, who told the historical tales, were entrusted with 178 prime stories."[11] Minstrel brotherhoods existed in Europe during the Middle Ages: the Strasburg "Brotherhood of the Crown," and that formed by St. Nicholas of Vienna in 1288.

In Germany, there was a Guild of Meistersingers at Nuremberg which had three divisions—apprentices (students), companions (neophytes), and masters (initiates). There were actually five grades in the Guild of Meistersingers:

1. Pupils.

2. School of Friends (who had to know something of the rules of music and song, and a certain number of tones and poems).

3. Singers (had to be able to sing without error a given number of songs and poems).

4. Poets (had to be able to make new poems based on the old models, as the new ever builds upon the old). The task was to conserve the elements of the past that

had enduring worth, and those elements which were a hindrance were left behind.

5. Masters (invented a new tone and a new mode). The master had to make his/her own rules and then follow them. Each was to be a creator in their own right. They were expected to give free expression to their own genius but in strict adherence to the laws of his/her own being. The individual had to be able to accommodate the changing needs of the creative spirit.

The early initiate bards sang often of heavenly realms, cloaking their experiences of these realms in poetry, song, and story. The "dreamsongs" were often their accounts of the inner-plane activities. The master song was one that was inspired from sources higher than the earth.

Training in the bardic traditions took two basic forms. The first was an inherited training. There could be a loose "blood" relationship with the teacher, or the training was passed on from one member of the family to the next by word of mouth. The second was through apprenticeship with a group or an individual. This could be formal or informal instruction and initiation.

The formal apprenticeship really does not exist any more in the world. An example of formal training, however, could be seen through the zenza of Japan. The student was called "minarai," and in their first period of training they worked with a master for about six to twelve months. This period was called "the act of entering the gate of apprenticeship." The Master would give the student an artistic name.

The second period of training would last two to three years. During this time, the student was never to write any stories down. They had to recite the stories verbatim until they had discovered for themselves the "secret" of the story. When the student knew the story well enough, only then were they allowed to work away from the master and interpret the stories and songs in their own way.

It is not unusual to find that the students were given instruction in philosophy, astrology, and healing in conjunction with the musical and storytelling training. The students had to learn the proper formulas and effects and then learn to use the formulas in their own manner. (In the next chapter, there are some charts on the effects of musical harmony when applied to the storytelling process.)

In an informal apprenticeship, the process was a little different. There was still training in many esoteric subjects, and the training often lasted a period of one to three years in most areas of the world. This is reflected in the teaching of Jesus Christ and the Apostles. Some informal apprentices have lasted as long as ten years. Usually the student must either only listen or repeat word for word what the Master recites and tells. Through imitation, the student learns the material and how to develop resonance with an audience. Only then is the student allowed to perform on his or her own.

In most societies, the bard had to be able to draw upon a wealth of tales and myths to suit the occasion and adapt it to the understanding of the audience. Some of the stories, myths, and tales common to all of the bardic traditions can be placed in the following categories:

- Stories of the young and old.
- Stories of true loves and false.
- Stories of riddles, tricksters, and rogues.
- Stories of the Wise Fool.
- Stories of heroes (historical and mythical).
- Stories of wonder and magic.
- Stories of shapeshifting.
- Stories of non-human life.

- Stories of fooling the devil.
- Stories of quests for wisdom.
- Stories of ghosts and ancestors.
- Stories of birth and creation.
- Stories of death and the world's end.
- Stories of morality and behavior.
- Stories of the relationship of the divine with humanity.

THE MAGIC IN MYTHS AND TALES

The transmission of tales serves a number of functions. First, tales entertain. Second, they endow a society's or person's position with greater value. Third, they serve to educate. They help to maintain and delineate proper behavior. They cloak mysteries, teachings, and energies that could otherwise be profaned. They help us to find meanings in our lives.

The importance of myths and tales in the evolutionary process of a people or individual has been overlooked in modern society. Children in more ancient times were schooled in the listening arts. The Xhosa and Zulu of South Africa are still trained in listening and narrating at an early age. The "ibota" is a storytelling event within the celebration of a family in Africa.

Because they were so often imbued with a dynamic thoughtform of energy and phrased in such a manner so as to elicit a specific effect, the tales and myths of the ancient bards were magical. They were spellbinding. "For a story to truly hold a child's attention, it must entertain him and arouse his curiosity. But to enrich his life, it must stimulate his imagination; help him to develop his intellect and to clarify his emotions; be attuned to his anxieties and aspirations; give full recognition to his difficulties, while at the same time suggesting solutions to the problems which perturb him."[12]

In traditional Hindu medicine, tales are given to the individual to meditate upon. The tale gives form to a particular problem. The individual must find his or her own solutions, inspired by the circumstances within the tale. The content of the tale reflects the inner conflicts of the individual. The person "giving" the tale must attune to the individual, infuse the tale with the right images so that it will resonate with the individual.

Because of the symbolic language within myths and tales, they can be used for two kinds of magic. The first is a form of sympathetic magic. This is reflected in the phrase "like attracts like." The images are linked to archetypal energies that can be released into the individual's life. Through a form of mythic immersion, in which the individual places himself or herself into the scenario while in a meditative state, the energies associated with the tale are released.

This release occurs in a unique manner, and yet will follow the pattern of the story. This is the source of the power behind many of the ancient ritual plays. This release may stimulate certain physical life circumstances symbolized by the story or it may simply trigger "magical enlightenment." The storyteller, through his/her technique, induces an altered state of consciousness and a dynamic resonance and/or response in the audience. The audience experiences the story, much in the same manner as getting caught up within a movie or good book. The difference is that the words and images are chosen and expressed so as to elicit effects on the emotional, mental and spiritual consciousness of the individual.

The second form of magic can be called impartial, and it is used more often for individual enlightenment. In this form, the part stands for the whole. The tale tells only part of the story, but it reveals enough that the individual is capable of making the leap to its true understanding. The second form is more subtle, and it actually may have a variety of significances. Many of the ancient parables, especially those found within the New Testament scriptures, have as many as seven interpretations. It is the last and deepest which encompasses all of the others. (Refer to the section in this chapter "Mysteries in the Christian Parables.")

This technique of magical enlightenment was often used to prevent the deeper esoteric truths from being profaned. Each individual had to search out the significance themselves and find the applications to his/her own life circumstances.

Myths and tales, like dreams, can touch us on all levels. They provide a structure and a tool for life direction. The ancient bards recognized this and utilized it to open higher visions, to restore health, and to overcome obstacles. Myths and tales help us to deal with the individual predicaments of our lives. In most myths and tales, good and evil are present, and both have their attractions.

There are differences, however, between myths and such stories as fairy tales and parables. Myths are often broader and the divine interplay of life is more apparent. Fairy tales or simple stories take those same ideas and translate them into terms for the average person. The ancient bards often translated the myths into a working and understandable model for the average person, resulting in our fairy tales and folklore. Today we have the task of using them to build new mythologies or new expressions of the old. The modern bard must learn to use stories, poems, songs, and words to form a bridge to the more complex archetypes that once were reflected only in ancient mythologies.

There is within the ancient power of the Word an operative law, sometimes called the Law of Correspondence: "As above, so below; as below, so above."[13] Simply, what we do on one level affects us on all others. As we learn to use the tales and stories and imbue them with greater power and significance, we open to that archetypal energy more fully. Although the fairy tale may be simpler and often more comprehensible, it can open us to those more primal energies.

All tales and myths speak to us in symbols. As we will learn, there are specific ways of using sacred sound to imbue the images with greater force. As we learn to do so, not only do they come to life for us, but we can learn to bring those same energies to life in others. We free the archetypes behind the images to manifest within our lives.

MYSTERIES IN THE CHRISTIAN PARABLES

(The parables in the Christian Scriptures can be placed in six categories, reflecting the lessons and stages of true unfoldment.)

Parables of the Old and New

These are parables that teach of the process of change and building upon the old. Some examples include such parables as "New Wine and the Old Wine," "Treasures New and Old," and "The New Patch on the Old Garment."

Parables of the Preparation for Discipleship

These depict the qualities and dedication necessary for discipleship. It includes such parables as "Pearl of a

Great Price," "The Hidden Treasure," "The Mustard Seed," and "The Leaven."

Parables as Symbols of Discipleship

These seven tales depict the lessons associated with the qualities needed to move from discipleship to higher initiation. Four of these were told in large crowds, and three were given to the Apostles in private. They are "The Chief Seats," "The Pharisee and the Publican," "The Laborers and the Hours," "Parable of the Talents," "Parable of the Pounds," "The Good Samaritan," and "The Parable of the Sower."

Parables of Obstacles Toward Attainment

These depict pitfalls and obstacles that the individual may encounter upon the path. They include such parables as "The Unmerciful Servant," "The Young Ruler," "The Rich Fool," "Lazarus and the Rich Man," "The Prodigal Son," "The Lost Sheep," and "The Rejected Cornerstone."

Parables Teaching the Process of Regeneration

These involve the higher teachings of alchemy, discipleship, and testing upon the initiatory path. Some examples include the parables of "The Barren Fig Tree," "The Last Judgment," and "The Parable of the Tares."

Parables of Initiation

These are the parables containing deeper esoteric significance and they involve words and images symbolic of these deeper truths. They are for those who have found the path of discipleship and were ready for the deeper work of attainment. They include the teachings of the kundalini and the primal creative forces. They include the parables of "The Wise and Foolish Virgins," "The Great Supper," "The Wedding Garment," and "The Wedding of the King's Son."

Through the Biblical parables, definite steps in occult development are revealed. They contain words, phrases, and images symbolic of "The Way of Evolution" (for the masses) and "The Way of Initiation" (for the few).

NOTES TO CHAPTER FIVE

1. This Hassidic tale has been told in many ways by many people. This particular version has its source in John Shea, "Theology and Autobiography: Relating Theology to Lived Experience,"*Commonweal*, June 16, 1978, pp. 358–362. It is retold by Jane Yolen in *Folktakes From Around the World* (New York: Pantheon Books, 1986), p. 10.

2. Jane Yolen, Ed. *Favorite Folktales From Around the World*. (New York: Pantheon Books, 1986) p. 11.

3. Ann Pellowski, *The World of Storytelling* (New York: Bowker, 1977) p. 9.

4. Eino Friberg, trans. *The Kalevala*. (Finland: Otava Publishing, 1988) p. 41, lines 1–70.

5. Homer, *The Odyssey*, trans. Albert Cook (New York: W.W. Norton, 1974) lines 150–155 and 325–371.

6. W.H.D. Rouse, *The Great Dialogues of Plato*. (New York: Mentor Books, 1956) Book III, pp. 182–217.

7. Ovid, *Metamorphoses,* trans. Arthur Golding (New York: MacMillan, 1965) Book X, Lines 1–151; pp. 249–253.

8. Richard McKeon, ed. *Basic Works of Aristotle: Politics* (New York: Random House, 1941) Book VIII, Chapter 3, pp.1306–1308.

9. Cicero, *De Oratore*, trans H. Rackman and E.W. Sutton "The Making of an Orator" (London: Harvard University Press, 1942) Book I, p.p. 160–204.

10. Joseph Campbell. "Exploring Myth with Joseph Campbell," *The Inward Light*, Nos. 8–9; Winter 1976–1977; p. 50.

11. Jane Yolen, ed. *Folktales From Around the World* (New York: Pantheon Books, 1986) p. 11.

12. Bruno Bettelheim, *The Uses of Enchantment* (New York: Random House, 1975) p. 5.

13. Three Initiates, *The Kybalion* (Chicago: Yogi Publication Society, 1940) pp.28–30 and pp. 113–136. The Law of Correspondence is also the second sentence of the Emerald Tablet of Hermes Trismegistus: "What is below is like that which is above; and what is above is like that which is below: to accomplish the miracle of one thing."

CHAPTER SIX

The Art of
Magical Storytelling

There are many theories of the origins of storytelling. It may have arisen out of a form of playful, self-entertainment. It may have arisen as a means to explain the phenomenal world. It may have arisen as a means to honor the supernatural, or even out of a need to communicate experiences to others.

Regardless of its origins, the art of magical storytelling lies deep within us all. The task now is to search it out and to make it grow once more. This task involves awakening the creative imagination, for the heart of the tradition lies in the imagination. We must develop the power to evoke emotion (together with spiritual conviction) by imbuing the images with greater power and significance. Today's magical storyteller must develop a deeper understanding of symbols and people, and he/she must also develop a stronger sense of selectivity and discrimination in their application.

In her book *The World of Storytelling,* Anne Pellowski defines storytelling as "the art or craft of narration of stories in verse and/or prose, as performed or led by one person before a live audience: the stories may be spoken, chanted or sung, with or without musical, pictorial and/ or other accompaniment, and may be learned from oral, printed or mechanically recorded sources; one of its purposes must be that of entertainment."

Magical storytelling is the use of storytelling to open to expanded perceptions, enlightenment, and magical states of consciousness. Anyone who has experienced an effective guided meditation has experienced a form of magical storytelling. The meditation utilizes images and scenarios designed to elicit specific effects. This is why the ancient occult technique of pathworking (most often found in Qabalistic practices) is so effective in the process of unfoldment.[1]

Magical storytelling awakens the child within us that still remembers and recognizes the subtle energy plays of life. It helps us to "become again as a little child" as Biblical scripture encourages. Everything has life to a child. Stones are alive. Streams speak a gurgling language and have a will because the water is flowing. Animals think or are inhabited by a spirit. Things can feel and act, and although parents may say otherwise, the child knows differently. Unfortunately, this true knowledge becomes buried.

Magical storytelling provides a simple and emotional appeal to that child within us. It stirs long dormant feelings, and it can quicken our compassion and sympathy. It offers wit and wisdom, while inspiring our imaginations once more. It encourages us to trust that the small acts we perform in our lives are very important. It inspires us to action. There are many victims and seekers in the magical tales of the world. Bad luck must be dealt with; it can't be ignored. Stories can teach the responsibility we have of *acting* in our life circumstances, giving greater depth of meaning to the axiom that "evil prospers when good people do nothing."

Magical storytelling helps us to uncover solutions to our problems. Internal processes are brought forth and made more comprehensible by the story events. It helps to translate psychic realities into images that will assist understanding. While the symbolic interpretation of the tales may be overstated (and to many people may seem inconsequential), it does help train us in seeing hidden significances and patterns which can carry over into our day-to-day life perceptions. While many may contest individual interpretations, we must remember that every tale has the potential of resonating uniquely within each of us. And that is where it reveals its true power.

THE FORMULA FOR MAGICAL STORYTELLING

Everyone can tell stories, but the ancient mystics and bards would infuse them with specific images to elicit even more dynamic effects. They would meditate upon them and then vocalize in a manner to most suit the audience for whom the story was directed. An effective magical storyteller often describes an inner state of consciousness through the images and the actions of characters. The story becomes a mirror reflecting an aspect of the inner world.

Magical storytelling is an interpretive art and it can be applied to all professions. It can be used to establish rapport, to illustrate points, to impart information, to create a mood, and to build climaxes. It is a form of aesthetic and spiritual communication that changes in accordance with the circumstances of the telling.

There is a large realm of material to draw upon for the individual wishing to learn this powerful art. The more tales that you become familiar with, the wider the resonance with the audience. There is a plethora of myths, legends, epics, fables, parables, ballads, anecdotes, folk-lore and fairy tales to choose from.

Because of the wide selection available, deciding which stories to adapt to the magical process is not always easy. Begin by reading or re-reading those myths and tales that you enjoyed as a child. They obviously touched you for a reason, and may reflect energies intimate to your life. Look to your ancestry and race, explore the myths and tales associated with those cultures. If you practice a particular religion, explore the myths and tales associated with it. Begin by choosing tales that are tied to an aspect of your life.

Any tale that you decide to use in the magical process should have three touchstones:

Universality

The idea expressed within the tale is potentially interesting to everyone. It may evoke a common emotional response or it may touch on a common experience to all or most of the audience. It has or can be made to have relevance to the life experience of most people.

Individuality

This is the fresh approach you apply to the subject of the story. It includes your own choice of words, images and method of organizing the events to elicit the effect you most wish to create.

Suggestion

The magical storytelling should leave the audience with something to do. It suggests enough so that the individual's own imaginative faculties can find correlations and applications to his or her own individual life. Pointing out the significance or rubbing the moral in can destroy the magical aspect. Keep in mind that the story is a catalyst for change, but the individual must take the catalyst and respond in his or her own fashion. The audience must find its own application of the story.

Having chosen your story, analyze and edit it for your own purposes. While doing the analysis, try to understand the people. Identify their major traits, motivations, relationships to others, their purposes, etc. Develop an arresting introduction, and determine a variety of sensory images that could be employed. Limit its length so that it lasts five to seven minutes. Determine ways in which you can adapt this same story to different audiences, taking into consideration language and style as well as the theme itself.

Always be aware of the theme of any story you decide to work with. Often, the speaking occasion may determine the theme. You may wish to develop a list of stories that fall under the same theme category or which can be adapted to suit a particular theme. There is an old tale that comes from the Nupe of Nigeria called "The Talking Skull." I have adapted this story for use in such themes as "The Importance of Reticence in Speech," "Considerations in Making a Name for Yourself," "The Power of our Words," "The Effects of Words upon the Health of the Body" and in others. Many folktales and legends are easily adapted for the magical storytelling process.

Most stories in the magical storytelling process follow a particular structure. The content may vary, but the form rarely does. The story must have a beginning. Most often, it very simply states the who, what, when and where aspects of the story itself. There is an initial incident which sets the tone for the development that follows, leading to a climax and a conclusion.

For any story, memorize the sequence. The idea is to develop a flow without memorizing the story word for word. There must be a fluency to the story in its telling, one that comes alive through both verbal and non-verbal techniques. The storytelling process may seem easy and spontaneous, but as with any art it is practiced and honed with each telling.

Laws of Form

There are resources to help you improve your magical storytelling. For example, Axel Olrick wrote an article called "The Epic Laws of Folk Narrative."[2] In this article he outlined the laws of form as they applied to epics. Many of these same laws can be applied in creating a magical formula for the storytelling process, one that will elicit a more dynamic effect:

Law of Opening

Don't begin with sudden action. Move from calm to excitement.

A traditional story hour opening is the lighting of a candle. This serves as a call to attention. (This will be explored further at the end of this chapter in "An Exercise in Magical Storytelling.")

Law of Closing

Don't end abruptly. Move from excitement to calm. Use humor or surprise or twists as a final play of magical energy through the story. The closing is often determined by the story and its particular theme. Some end with a nonsense or rhymes. There is also a ceremonial ending which is often applied in formal storytelling hours. This can be the extinguishing of the story hour candle after the making of a wish, or it can be any other ceremony developed for the occasion.

Law of Repetition
This is used for emphasis. It builds tension and helps to fill out the narrative. Events or situations are often repeated three times, as three is a magical number, associated with the rhythms of the awakening child and new birth.

Law of Three
This law often appears in myths, legends, and tales with great frequency. Spells are repeated three times, there are three objects, three people, etc. Three is especially strong in Greek, Celtic, Teutonic and Semitic tales. In India, the tales often have the Law of Four as its key rhythm.

The Law of Contrast
Sometimes this is called the law of two to a scene. Two is often the maximum number in a scene that are active. There may be others, but they are often nothing more than onlookers. There is usually a contrasting polarity which resonates with primal polarities deep within our own consciousness (young and old, male and female, large and small). It also enables interaction that is more easily relayed verbally.

Law of Logic
There must be a theme influencing the plot in the magical storytelling process. This logic may not be the logic of the natural world, but it must apply to the world of the story itself whether it is the world of animism, the world of magic, or any other world. This logic makes possible a union between the actual and the ideal. It begins to reveal a means of bridging the two worlds together—either by having them come together in the story itself or by bridging the story world to the real world of the audience.

Law of a Single Strand

Don't go back and fill in details. Allow the background to unfold within the dialogue of the tale itself. Let it flow with a progressive series of movements that lead logically to the conclusion, whether predictable or surprising.

ADDING MAGIC TO THE STORY

The first step to turning a normal storytelling into a magical one is to learn as much about the story and its images as possible. Work with the symbology. How have those images and symbols been used in the past? What are they representative of? What is the secret behind the story? What does it teach? Try and discover as many significant aspects of the story as you can. Write them down. These significant aspects will help you find ways of applying this story more appropriately to the events of your own life.

Meditate upon the story. Perform a type of mythical immersion by placing yourself in the events of the story and allow yourself to go through them, as you would in a normal daydream. Keep in mind that guided imagery, such as that which is found in tales and myths, can lead us to those more archetypal forces behind the imagery. This kind of magical journey assists us in merging our finite minds with the infinite mind of the universe.

This mythical immersion is sometimes called a magical journey. It is a variation of the previously mentioned pathworking technique of the Qabala. In this technique, the imagery of the story is adapted to appear as if you are going on a journey into the circumstances of the story itself. You allow yourself to relax and then to visualize yourself going on this magical journey, one which places you within the events of the story as one of its characters. For example, we could use the tale of Jason and the Argonauts as a basis for a magical journey by simply substituting ourselves for Jason or any other character within the tale.

When we create a magical journey through the storytelling process, we create a series of images and actions that we play out within our mind while in a relaxed (altered) state of consciousness. The relaxed state enables us to activate greater inner energies and awareness. The magical journey will resonate with us at the level to which we can respond.

In magical storytelling, we utilize the imagination in a concentrated, controlled, and directed manner in order to elicit specific responses either in our own lives or the lives of our audience. Thus, it is important to understand the effects of the symbols and images that you utilize within your stories.

The imagination is one of our greatest assets. It can be used to enhance and augment our lives. It is the directing of specific images in a controlled process (meditation, pathworking, guided journeys, creative visualization, and magical storytelling) to manifest specific effects within our physical life circumstances.

Make sure you use your own imagination in the myths, tales, and stories you use. Adapt them. Construct them to meet your particular needs. A degree of spontaneity is vital. Through the years I have led many people through guided meditations and magical stories, and no matter how many times I have used a particular meditation, it never comes out the same way twice. There are always variations and adaptations according to what the audience responses were prior to the meditative work. Yes, there is a basic outline, but within the confines of that outline there must be a flexibility to adjust it to more fully meet the needs of the audience.

Before you use a guided imagery meditation or a magical storytelling, know exactly what kind of responses the audience can expect to experience as a result of encountering the images of your story while in an altered state. If you have placed yourself in a position of being the meditation facilitator, you must keep in mind the responsibility you have to the other participants. It is a good idea to let them know what they can expect as a result of performing the exercise. They should be informed of possible effects of the images you will use so that they can choose whether or not to participate.

The meditation facilitator and the magical storyteller are teachers, and as such there is a responsibility to know the hows and whys and the effects of what you involve your audience or students in. There are many out in the public sector "teaching" some aspect of metaphysics with little more experience than having read a book or two and learned a simple meditational technique. They do not always have the depth of knowledge nor the sensitivity to recognize how the audience will respond. They can lead individuals into experiences that are disruptive and possibly even traumatizing.

Learning as much as possible about the symbology of the story—and about symbology in general—will help you to use it more responsibly and more effectively. Your knowledge will empower the storytelling process. Learn about the archetypal symbols behind the imagery of everyday life. Perform the storytelling or meditation for yourself alone, and do it often, so that you can experience the effects personally before you involve others.

Guided imagery and active imagination—as applied through the magical storytelling process—do produce altered states of consciousness in which the archetypal energies operating behind and through the imagery will emerge. Control is the key to working with this process. Although the storytelling may seem fluid and spontaneous, it should be practiced and prepared for on all levels. Only with control can the images within the myths and stories take the individual into the sacred areas of their beings to facilitate transformations. It is the personal inner reality which is of significance, and if we are to experience our innermost reality through magical storytelling in a creative and healthy manner, we must maintain control.

Before you use magical storytelling as a meditative experience, know exactly—step by step—what you wish to have happen on this journey. Construct and adapt the tale so that the outcome will meet your own unique purpose. Initially stick to it. You will find that as you gain experience, you will become more spontaneous. Spontaneity is vital, but control is even more vital.

Experiment with gesture and voice before you ever use it with others. Concentrate upon the words you use within the story. Learn to use them and not waste them. Have them ready at hand. Each time you practice the story, visualize it having the appropriate effects upon the audience. With each practice, you create a magical thoughtform that will give your storytelling even greater magic when actually used.

The use of visualization and creative imagination enables the magical storyteller to be more than someone who merely relates events. Through the energy of the story, you project vivid mental pictures that dynamically resonate with the audience. Stress the key images within the story.

Any oral message involves both verbal and non-verbal aspects. Both have great importance, but that which is non-verbal can transcend the spoken or written. This includes body motion and posture, gestures, and the amount of eye contact. The ability to create an empathic response also depends partly on breath control, the ability to project, the rate and pause of the speech, its intelligibility, and the vocal quality. This book cannot teach you all of those aspects, but they must be considered in the magical storytelling process. Most colleges and adult education centers teach classes on speech and oral interpretation, which can assist you in developing these aspects even more fully. Most libraries also have storytelling groups who can provide assistance within these aspects.

What differentiates the magical storyteller from the average person who tells a story is that the former has delved into the hidden significances of the story imagery. The magical storyteller understands the significance of the power of the voice and its ability to be used to resonate with deeper levels of another's psyche. The magical storyteller understands that everything said, every gesture made, every aspect of the storytelling process is a tool for invoking energy and for eliciting an altered state of consciousness that can be utilized for purposes other than mere entertainment. Everything within the storytelling process is imbued with significance. The storytelling then becomes a creative manifestation of the power of the Word.

MAGICAL-MUSICAL JOURNEYS

Music and tones can facilitate the process of magical storytelling. The can help us enter into new levels of consciousness. Tones trigger dramatic effects within the body and consciousness. If we learn to combine the tones with specific imagery, we can begin to touch new levels and dimensions of life. We can use the combination of tones and images to access other planes of awareness.

Musical tones can be incorporated into meditational work to facilitate a deeper response within the consciousness. Music is now being composed specifically to elicit effects that correspond to the guided imagery. The music is chosen because it resonates with the innate energy of the imagery. They reinforce each other, magnifying the effects.

When music is added in the proper manner to the images we are creating, the effects are accelerated and amplified. Just as an artist can illustrate the contents of a book, adding color and value to it, the magical storyteller can utilize tones to enhance the value of the developmental process. Finding tones and combinations of tones to release even greater energies, the metaphysician becomes an artist. He or she paints in musical tones.

This method of tone painting was common in more ancient times—especially in the recital of poetry designed to create a mantra or litany effect. Each stanza of the poem was often recited on the same tone. Sometimes, three different tones were used: one for the introduction, one for the main body and another for the conclusion. In some societies, a drum was used to set the tone and rhythm of the poem or story.

In more modern times, this process of tone painting can be seen in the movies, on T.V. and within theatres. The musical score is used to enhance the action upon the screen or stage. It involves the audience more actively, drawing them into the experience.

This is what the "New Age" genre of music is leading to. It can be used to enhance many works. Many people are beginning to explore music and incorporate it into their meditation groups. Unfortunately, some are not as cognizant of the effects, and they often choose the music simply because it is labeled "New Age" and not because it suits the imagery. In cases such as this it will interfere with accessing deeper levels of consciousness. It is distracting and the effects of the imagery within the meditational work is severely limited. We have all experienced grade "B" movies where the musical score just did not fit the action upon the screen. It is tremendously distracting.

If we employ music that fits, if we relate tones to the specific activities of the magical journey, the effects are amplified. It stimulates deeper emotions and greater associations on all levels of the psyche. The following illustrations and descriptions portray some of the spiritual and emotional responses to musical harmony. These can be applied to tone painting in the magical storytelling process. We simply match the tone(s) with the emotional and spiritual response depicted within the story.

RESPONSE TO MUSICAL HARMONIES

(The responses given here can be evoked in any key. For simplification, the key of C major and minor is depicted.)

The Perfect Octave

This elicits a feeling of rest. It is the energy of union, the male and female coming into a new wholeness of expression. It is the linking of poles for a higher and more balanced expression.

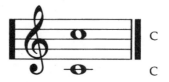

The Fifth

This will stimulate the feelings of movement and power. It can awaken feelings of new life coming forth. It is the power of the microcosm and of rebirth within it.

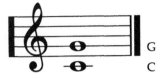

G
C

The Third

The third is a interval that is simple and uncluttered. When used with magical storytelling, it leaves room for some embellishment by the individual. It awakens feelings of compatibility and the beginning of resonance.

E
C

The Fourth

This is a dyad that announces something new. It awakens feelings of movement and hints of an entrance. It can also awaken feelings of being controlled. It touches the heart and rings within it, and that can make some people feel uneasy.

F
C

The Seventh

The seventh awakens feelings of distance and the need for resolution. It opens feelings of anticipation and drama, of something being incomplete and unresolved. It also can be used to hint at a new sense of direction an opening, or an awakening.

B

C

The Minor Third

This is the interval of sadness and depression. It touches the lower emotional responses. It hints at indecision, vagueness, and lack of direction. It implies that disharmony is about to unfold, even though it hasn't yet. It stimulates that vague sense of doom, and foreshadows failure or disharmony.

E-flat
C

The Minor Seventh

This interval can be used to awaken feelings of discord and drama. It stimulates a sense of friction. There is a feeling of incompletness that comes with it. It is a threshhold tone. It can be used to awaken feelings of loneliness and distance. It creates the feeling that new and unexpected doors are about to open.

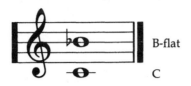

B-flat

C

The Major Chord

This chord can be used to stimulate feelings of joy and completeness. It implies movement and lack of inhibition. It is positive, resolving, and uplifting. It promotes feelings of fulfillment and potential.

C
G
E
C

The Minor Chord

The minor chord is earthing to the energies. It brings the experience of storytelling down to a level to which the individual can respond. It can be used for feelings of gloom and sadness. It draws the listener into greater sympathetic or empathic participation in the experience.

C
G
E-flat
C

The Augmented Chord

The augmented chord builds a sense of uncertainty in the listener. It activates feelings of uneasiness without anything substantial to base it upon. It can be used to increase tension.

It hints at events moving even further than originally anticipated.

C
G-sharp
E
C

The Diminished Chord

The diminished chord can also be used to create tension and excitement. It draws the action of the story closer to the listener, as if to hint at something impending. It creates a feeling of strain. It can create a kind of ethereal anticipation of new or renewed activity. (The example below is a diminished 5th in a C chord.)

C
G-flat
E
C

Music is a tremendous aid to the achievement of altered states of consciousness. It can be used to help evoke associations, memories, and thoughts associated with the imagery in magical storytelling. It can be used to awaken new creativity. It is a reinforcement of symbolic associations in the magical journey. It has great import in all ritual aspects of storytelling.

This is why those of the more esoteric bardic traditions were schooled in music and could play some musical instrument. Each society had its own key instrument. In Brazil, it was the berimba. The harp was the primary instrument in the Teutonic, Anglo-Saxon, Norse, and Icelandic traditions. The lyre was associated with the Greek bards, but even they were distinguished from the Greek Masters who played the kithara. The playing of a musical instrument facilitated the student's understanding of the principles of the power of the Word. Regardless of the instrument, by learning to create music with it the individual learned to empower the words and create even more moving responses. The bardic student learned to combine words and music to alter energy at its most intimate and complex levels. The instrument became a symbol and a tool of this ability.

Musical instruments fall into one of four categories: strings, wind, percussion, and keyboard. All have application to the magical storytelling process. Many believe they cannot ever learn to play an instrument, but there are those which can be played without extensive study. Even if you cannot play an instrument, understanding some of the symbolic aspects will assist you in deciding on recorded music that you can apply to your own magical storytelling.

The following instruments are by no means the easiest to play, but they have great applicability to the magical storytelling process. They can also be expensive. However, it is possible to buy an inexpensive synthesizer which will duplicate the sounds of these instruments, thus enabling you to apply them to your own tone-painting activities in your magical stories.

LYRE

The seven-stringed lyre is a symbol of the mysticism of the universe. Each string is related to a mood of humanity, to a subtle body, to one of the seven major planets and to one of the seven planes of life. Each string has reflected within it an aspect of the human soul and the laws of science and art.

The lyre has been associated with many ancient masters and myths. It was the first instrument of Apollo. It was passed on to his son Orpheus who could animate the inanimate with its music. Students of Pythagoras were trained in its use, and it is said that they used it in their travels to deeply touch the souls of those they met. If a child were crying, they would play a sequence of tones to calm it. If someone expressed anger, they would use specific chords to dissipate it. If there were illnesses, the tones were played to restore balance.

It was believed that Pythagoras could walk into a town, a room, or a building and transpose its structure into a musical combination. This reflects many of the oriental teachings of how energy is affected by physical structures and environments in relation to the natural flow of energy.

The lyre is an instrument that links the physical with all other dimensions of life. It can induce altered states of consciousness for any purpose. It is a powerful tool in magical storytelling. It calms emotional and mental states of unrest and imbalance. It moves the heart chakra into activity. It awakens the energies of the planets. It can be used to balance all of the chakras.

When used as a symbol for meditation or in the magical storytelling process, it offers protection and harmony. It serves as a call or a signal to the energies of Apollo, god of the Sun in Greek mythology. It is a symbol that can be used to awaken prophecy. It is also a call—especially when used in magical storytelling—to the Archangel Haniel who is the patroness of the arts.

HARP

The harp has been having a resurgence of popularity in the metaphysical field. It is a variation of the lyre. Legend tells of its origin being suggested by the hunting bow. Its predecessor, the lyre, has been depicted in almost every society. Pictures of it are found within the Egyptian hieroglyphics.

The harp serves an important function in the art of magical storytelling. It has the capacity for raising the energy of an individual. It calms the emotions and links the heart chakra with the crown. It is cleansing to the entire auric field. Because of that, it was frequently used in healing temples and rooms. Medieval nobility would bring harpists to play for members of a family that were convalescing after an illness. The harp hastens the healing process.

In many of the druid teachings, the harpist would dedicate his or her harp to the Mother Earth. It became an instrument for higher consciousness and healing, to be used only by one initiated into the higher teachings. Today it can still be used to raise consciousness, induce altered states, quicken the healing process, and bring joy to the lives of those who play or listen. The harp is an instrument that one learns to play by playing it. Yes, it can be taught, but simply sitting and learning to create pleasing sounds with it awakens the inner muse.

GUITAR

The folk guitar is a more modern form of the harp. It is easily portable, and it has the same capacity for healing as the harp and the lyre. It can be used for the relaying of ballads and tales through song. It has a versatility not often found within many of the harps.

KEYBOARD INSTRUMENTS

Keyboard instruments are also effective in the magical storytelling process. Most keyboards fall into one of three categories: piano, organ, or synthesizer. The piano combines string tones and percussion, and because of this it can be used in any way that a percussion instrument can.

The bass section of the piano can be used to establish a rhythm that corresponds to the rhythm of the story. The upper sections or higher notes can be used to produce melodies that elicit specific emotional and mental responses. They can be used to stimulate harmony and lift consciousness to new heights. The piano has the capability of incorporating rhythm, melody and harmony, in accordance with the story itself.

The organ is an instrument of sheer sonic power. It has a capacity for creating forced resonance or entrainment in any area in which it is used. The physical vibration triggered by the organ literally enters the listeners' bodies, permeating and shaking responses from them. It can create unique inner experiences.

Synthesized music enables us to touch a variety of tones and timbres. Because it electronically reproduces sounds, it can be used to duplicate the sound of any instrument that you desire, and thus gives you a tremendous tool for tone-painting.

FLUTE

The flute is one of the oldest instruments in existence. It is part of the wind family. It has existed in various forms in different societies. It is considered one of the first instruments to enable humanity to connect with the beings of nature—the fairies, elves, devas, and others. Thus, it is powerfully effective when used with fairy tales in the magical storytelling process.

The flute is considered an extension of the body. It is played with the breath of life, the true creative force. It is often considered the instrument for the "Om," and it can be used to connect the individual with the consciousness of nature. Its primary drawback in the storytelling process is that you cannot speak and play it at the same time. You can, however, use recorded flute music very effectively. It also serves as an excellent introduction and conclusion in the storytelling process.

TIBETAN INSTRUMENTS

There is a renewed interest in the ancient Tibetan instruments. These instruments have great applicability to the magical storytelling process. They balance the hemispheres of the brain, thus paving the way for the imagery to be more easily received, and they serve as a signal, calling out to our deeper levels of consciousness.

Many of the musical instruments used in Tibetan healing and shamanic practices fall into the percussive category, but they are much more versatile. The bells, gongs, and cymbals are not only for rhythm but for creating unusual tones. Several of these are extremely effective healing instruments, with a capacity to shatter old patterns within the physical body and within the subtle bodies as well. What is known about them in Western society is only enough to make you wish to know more.

One of the most common is the Tibetan *bell and dorje* or thunderbolt. These are powerful ritual instruments in various shamanic and Buddhic practices. During religious ceremonies they are used in combination. The bell represents the female aspect of our energies—the yin side of us. This is called the prajna or wisdom aspect. The dorje represents the masculine or yang aspect. This is referred to as upaya, or the method for using the wisdom.

Bell and Dorge *Singing Bowl* *Cymbals*

As the bell is toned the dorje is handled in such a way as to circulate the energy about yourself. The two together help to restore the balance of male and female energy. In yoga, this would be comparable to opening the flow of prana known as the Ida and the Pingala, bringing them into balance in a central channel of energy that is referred to as the Susumna.

The bell and the dorje are a musical instrument, and have the capacity to elicit a wide variety of tones. There are also techniques of utilizing the mouth as an echo chamber in order to elicit a more "cosmic" sound. Their uses in the healing realm are yet to be completely explored. On a metaphysical level, they represent the union of wisdom and the method for attaining enlightenment.

The *Tibetan singing bowl* is one of the most powerful healing instruments of sound and vibration. Its uses are multiple. It is called a singing bowl or singing bell bowl because the exotic sound hovers in the air long after it has been played. Very little is known of its history, but it is generally recognized that it was created specifically to elicit tones for healing and ritual.

The bowls are made of seven metals. These include gold, silver, nickel, copper, zinc, iron, and antimony. Some sources say that the iron ore is from meteorites, but the veracity of that has yet to be proven.

Many of the bowls are 40-50 years old and were used by the Buddhist priests prior to the communist takeover in Tibet, but the bowls and their use date back centuries. The manner in which the metals are combined is not known, for the originals are all handmade to a specific formula known only to the masters. Since the Communist takeover of Tibet, the masters are not allowed to use the minerals in such a "frivolous" manner. Those that are coming into this country are coming predominantly through India. Some are being made in this country, and they are also effective. There is a difference though in the tones from the originals, which were handmade in the ancient tradition.

Each bowl has its own predominant tone which, when struck like a bell by a wooden dowel or striker, can be heard. What is unique about the bowls is that aside from its predominant tone, it sets off a series of overtones. The bowls are played by running a wooden wand along the edge of the bowl, encircling it. This is similar to running the finger around the edge of a crystal glass to make it sing. This method enables you to hear and feel the sound build until it permeates the surroundings.

The tones from the bowl balance the chakras, bring the subtle bodies into alignment, and create a balance between the right and left hemispheres of the brain. They shatter accumulating negative energy within the chakras and the aura. They resonate with every cell in the body to release blockages and restore balance. They restore the circular flow of energy within the aura.

Playing the bowls in a clockwise direction draws the tones into the body. The counterclockwise direction helps to draw out negativity. The bowls and their unique tones have been used to restore blood pressure, correct asthma and emphysema, and even rebuild adrenal function after failure from steroid intake. They open and balance the meridians of the body and they improve the synapse response in the brain. They have been used with hyperactive children and they can help stimulate the immune system.

The bowls are effective for meditation and magical storytelling as well. They can be used for personal work or group work. The tones from the bowl calm the mind and balance the body. They facilitate achieving an altered state of consciousness. Similar to listening to a rhythmic pattern of a drumbeat, the wave pattern of the bowl's tones enables one to achieve an alpha brain wave pattern—that of a relaxed, altered state.

The bowls can be used to induce trance conditions for vision quests. Many shamanic practitioners are utilizing them for magical journeys and as a vehicle for exploring many of the inner realms of their own consciousness. Meditating with the bowls and their subtle sounds attunes you to the universal sounds that surround us at all times. The singing of the bowls is an experience that everyone should have at least once. In healing and in magical practices, the singing bowls are a tool and a symbol of the infinite power and energy we can create by learning to work with sound, music, and tone.

The *Tibetan cymbals* are another effective tool for healing and for the magical storytelling process. When the cymbals are struck, they set off a crystal tone that calls every atom of being to attention. It cleanses the aura and relaxes the system, making it more receptive to the storytelling influence.

They are effective to use at the beginning and the end of a meditation or magical storytelling session. By beginning the session with them, there is a calming effect that facilitates resonance with the story symbols and images. Secondly, by ending the session with them, they leave the audience feeling calm, balanced, and refreshed.

AN EXERCISE IN MAGICAL STORYTELLING

Here is a summary of the necessary steps to take when preparing to tell a magical story.

1. Take time to meditate upon the story. Place yourself within the lead character's position. Then do the same thing with any other characters.

2. Explore all possibilities in the story. Make a list of everything it implies, along with ways you can apply it to your own life.

3. Visualize opportunities to tell the story or variations of it. Visualize others responding to it in an enthusiastic and positive fashion.

4. Listen to different types of music and find one that you can use as an appropriate background piece for the story. Practice telling the story with the music, so that the music enhances your words.

5. Are there any senses you can elaborate upon in the story? Are there any gestures that you can incorporate to augment the story and its elements?

6. Decide on a powerful introduction to be used in a more formal setting for the story. The traditional introduction is the lighting of a candle. In Israel, the opening of a story is preceded by the lighting of a fresh pipe of tobacco. In West Africa, in the latter part of the 19th century, the storytellers used a "song-net" upon which hung a variety of objects. The audience would then choose an object and a story would be told about it.

   Find new opening phrases. Instead of "Once upon a time..." or "Long, long ago..." use an original, such as "Long ago, when wishes were reality..." Be creative in your introduction. Make sure that it has significance to you. The more significance you can apply to the introduction, the more it will magically work for you.

   If you use the traditional lighting of a candle, see the lighting as a creative act. You are bringing into manifestation light where there was none. With your story, you will bring to light levels of consciousness and magic where none had been seen.

7. Have an appropriate conclusion. Don't leave the audience hanging. Don't overmoralize or overexplain. Let them find the significance as it applies to them. Close the story at its highest point, and then pause briefly. Use a closing ritual to wrap it all up and to assist the audience in returning to a normal state of consciousness. Have the audience make a wish before the candle is extinguished. Whatever the closing ritual, use it consistently. The more you use it, the more significant and powerful it becomes.

The following story is one that is very adaptable to the magical process. It has symbols and images which can be explored and expanded, adjusted and adapted, for a variety of situations. This version is taken from the book *Favorite Folktales From Around the World.*[3]

THE OLD LADY IN THE CAVE

There was once a man who was successful in all things. He had a fine wife, a loving family, and a craft for which he was justly famous. But still he was not happy.

"I want to know Truth," he said to his wife.

"Then you should seek her," she replied.

So the man put his house and all of his worldly goods in his wife's name (she being adamant on this point) and went out on the road a beggar for Truth.

He searched up the hills and down in the valleys for her. He went into small villages and large towns; into the forests and along the coasts of the great wide sea; into grim, dark wastes and lush meadows piled with flowers. He looked for days and for weeks and for months.

And then one day, atop a high mountain, in a small cave, he found her.

Truth was a wizened old woman with but a single tooth left in her head. Her hair hung down onto her shoulders in lank, greasy strands. The skin on her face was as brown as old parchment and as dry, stretched over prominent bones. But when she signalled to him with a hand crabbed with age, her voice was low and lyrical and pure and it was then that he knew he had found Truth.

He stayed a year and a day with her and learned all that she had to teach. And when the year and a day was up, he stood at the mouth of the cave ready to leave for home.

"My Lady Truth," he said, "you have taught me so much and I would do something for you before I leave. Is there anything you wish?"

Truth put her head to one side and considered. Then she raised an ancient finger. "When you speak of me," she said, "tell them I am young and beautiful!"

NOTES TO CHAPTER SIX

1. Refer to the author's previous work *Imagick: The Magic of Images, Paths and Dance* (St. Paul, MN: Llewellyn, 1989).

2. Axel Olrick, "The Epic Laws of Folk Narrative" in *Study of Folklore*, ed. Alan Dundes (New Jersey: Prentice-Hall, 1965).

3. From *Favorite Folktales From Around the World* by Jane Yolen. Copyright 1986 by Random House, Inc. Reprinted by permission of Pantheon Books, a division of Random House, Inc.

CHAPTER SEVEN

The Powers of the Poet-Seers

Art is one of the highest products of the imagination because it orders a disordered nature. For the magician and the musician, imagination and reality are of equal importance in life and are dependent upon each other. Through the poem-song the two are able to meet in a harmony that can resonate within the deepest levels of the soul.

Within poetry is the essence of the art found within the power of the Word. The poet strives for a union of sense and sound to elicit a specific effect. Many charms, spells, incantations, prayers, and forms of word magic find their success within the craft and art of poetry. Poetry is the writing of secret harmonies so that they can resonate on levels not often recognized. Poetry breathes life into imagined worlds.

In most societies, myths and tales can be found about individuals who were magical and poetic. In the Teutonic tradition, Odin was not only the father of the Norse pantheon, but he was the patron of poets as well. Isis and Osiris of the Egyptian mythology were patrons of music and poetry. Apollo in the Greek tradition was the god of prophecy and of music and art. Calliope was the muse of song and epic poetry. Talieson, of the Celtic tradition, was not only a shapeshifter but also was the master of poetry, magic, and the riddles of life. Mysticism and poetry were inseparable in times past. Gradually the poet-seer splits up into the figures of the prophet, the priest, the soothsayer, the mystagogue, and the poet as we know him.[1]

In poetry, the content and form are inseparable. They act together to achieve a magical effect. The patterned sound is what separates poetry from strict prose. It leaves much unsaid, allowing for individual resonance to occur. The words of the poem-song are selected with great care so as to guide the listener's response. Each word and phrase has a denotative (its more literal, dictionary definition) and connotative (an associated value, attitude or meaning) significance within the sound pattern of the entire poem. This allows the power of the words to activate energy on several levels simultaneously.

The ancient poet-seers were skilled in this manipulation of words to elicit specific effects. The tools of the poet were the techniques of working with words for various results. The prayers, songs, and incantations were magical poems, created through techniques now called rhetorical devices. Through these techniques the poet-seer awakened within the audience the dormant memory of the world of ideas. These techniques must be re-awakened and understood in the light of the magical process of the Word and not just as literary devices.

To the ancient seers, magic, music, and poetry were not mere pastimes. The success of their application was determined by the degree to which they were incorporated into the individual's way of life. Poetry, magic, and music are inseparable. They are tools to bridge the energies of imaginative worlds to the reality of day-to-day life.

Poetry is one of the few magical sciences that has retained its basic elements. Its structure, its content, and its sound values all add to the power of its words. The modern poet-magician must learn to employ all of these aspects. It is not enough just to turn a catchy phrase. Every aspect of the poem must be imbued with greater significance—from the words chosen, to their arrangement, to the overall form. Poems are not inherently magical. They are made magical by the way we create them and by the significance with which we imbue the elements used in that creation process.

There are many ways to classify poetry. For our purposes, we will create three distinctions: narrative, lyric, and magical. The first two are traditional classifications, and the third is one applicable to the magical process of life. All three are related to the power of the Word and the ancient bardic traditions.

A narrative poem tells a story or relates a series of events. Narrative poetry could be defined as a style of storytelling with the assistance of song. The oldest form of narrative poetry is the ballad. The ballad is simple in plot and very metrical in structure. The ballad was a part of many of the world's oral traditions in which esoteric ideas were presented within song. Ballads were meant to be accompanied by music. Many of the traditional ballads have no original or full version. The traditional ballads had a spirit beyond the letter of the song itself.

It is important to realize the significance of the ballad, beyond its entertainment aspect. "If a ballad could be restored to some non-existent original, or if a magical secret could be proven, they would be worthless shells. Restoration implies withdrawal of the vivifying spirit into another world, leaving only a shadow behind, or a ruin to be faked into a semblance of life. Such a restoration can only be made within ourselves, by bringing our own imagination alive within the traditional symbols."[2]

Another form of narrative poetry which can be used for magical effects is the epic tale. These poems, such as "Beowulf," usually have an elevated tone and a lofty language. They are easily adapted to a magical storytelling process.

The second classification of poetry is that which falls under the category of lyric. This was the common form used by the French troubadours. The lyric is typically a short poem shaped toward an emotional focal point. The emotional focus is the key to establishing audience resonance. The lyric's purpose is to achieve a response that can vary from gentle relaxation to passionate mysticism.

Lyric poetry often causes reflection. The ode, the sonnet, and the elegy fall into the lyric category. The original Greek odes were designed to be accompanied by music and a highly stylized dance, both powerful ways of invoking energy. The sonnet is more commonly recognized, and it is becoming a powerful magical tool in sacred psychology. It achieved its greatest popularity through Shakespeare, during the time of the Renaissance when language was richer, fuller, and deeper. It employs a scale and rhythm suitable for stimulating great resonance within deeper levels of the mind. It facilitates moving out of limiting syndromes and into new creative expressions. It will be explored in detail later within this chapter.

The other major classification that we are defining is a kind of magical poetry. It includes, but is not limited to, the previous two classifications. It employs literary devices and structures to a specific end—one that either evokes a new perception or invokes a new kind of energy in the individual's life. It is a conscious empowering and structuring of words, sounds, and music. It includes many of the ancient forms of mystical poetry, such as the "Odes of Solomon," the Hebrew psalms, and India's sacred song poems of Rig Veda. The construction and use of magical poem-songs will be explored at the end of this chapter.

STRUCTURING MAGICAL POETRY

In the writing of magical poetry, whether for the creation of a song or a prayer, the key is to make sure every aspect of the creation has meaning. The structure, the words, their rhythm, their arrangement—all must be explicitly and purposely chosen. The content and form are harmonized to have a particular effect.

An understanding of traditional literary devices can assist you in empowering your poetry with greater magic and an ability to resonate with other energies, both physical and subtle. These traditional literary devices often reflect magical laws and principles of the power of the Word.

In good poetry, (magical and otherwise) structure and content are always in harmony. The power of the poem depends greatly upon a blend of sounds and sense. The poet-seer strives for a union of sense and sound. This is known as tone color or the timbre of poetry. The poet-seer's choice and arrangement of the words determines the effect of the tone color. The emotional and astral energies of the content are enriched by the type of the color.

Creating the tone color involves combining words, vowels and consonants to help achieve particular effects. The choice and position of the words is often dictated by the way the sounds go together. Learning to create tone color in magical poetry requires learning to give words their full power. This means that techniques such as rhyme, alliteration, and onomatopoeia have great significance when applied to poetry that is designed to elicit a magical effect.

Conventional poetry has a pattern of stresses grouped in specified lengths. The stanzas (major units of thought or sound) are in a fixed pattern. There is a fixed line length, and there is usually an element of rhyme within each line, or a rhyme scheme within the entire poem.

Earlier we discussed the meistersingers, who had to learn to create new songs based upon old patterns. For magical poetry, we need to begin with fixed patterns. Have a set stanza length, a set line length and a rhyme scheme. Learn to use and integrate words and sounds within that pattern first before opening to other magical expressions.

Blank verse is an extension of the more conventional forms. It is not always rhymed, at least not at the end of the line. There are often internal rhymes. There is not a recurring stanza pattern, but there is usually a set line length. William Shakespeare's works contain excellent examples of incorporating acceptable rhythms of speech into blank verse.

One of the most difficult forms to use in creating magical poetry is free verse. This has been a recent addition to the realm of poetry, and in many ways it corresponds to the methods used by masters within the schools of the German meistersingers. In free verse, the individual invents a new structure, making his or her own rules and following them. It gives free expression to tan individual's creative genius, but in strict adherence to the laws of his/her own being. This kind of expression only occurs through discipline, the kind of discipline developed from working with the basics and the set patterns of the more conventional forms.

Many believe that free verse poetry has no set scheme or pattern—that it has no form or discipline. Often what is little more than a train of consciousness is passed off as free verse. To the poet-seer this is comical. The true poet-seer imposes a discipline without strict adherence to the traditional forms, and is able to go beyond them because he/she has learned to work through and master the traditional forms. You cannot work calculus if you do not know arithmetic.

Literary devices assist the poet-seer and the magical storyteller in creating a story that is allegorial, one that resonates beyond the surface level of meaning. For the poet-seer, the use of literary devices facilitates the resonance with the archetypal energy symbolized within the poem or story. The following is by no means a complete list of devices that the magical poet may employ, but it provides a starting point.

Alliteration

This is the repetition of the sound of certain letters. Knowing the significance of the letters will help the poet-seer to write a magical poem that goes beyond poetry and enters into the true force of incantations. The initial consonant sound is usually repeated. The initial consonant sound of a word or name is its cornerstone and can be used to activate certain spiritual and astrological influences.

Amplification and Repetition

In this device, words and phrases are emphasized through restatement. This ties into the Law of Three discussed in the previous chapter. The refrains of magical poetry, when repeated after each section, add power and intensity to the overall poem, prayer, or incantation. the power grows with each repetition so that by the final chorus the high point is achieved and the accumulated energy can be released to fulfill its function.

Anagrams

With this device, a word or phrase is made by transposing the letters. Magical names and spells can be created through this re-arrangement. It forces a more focused concentration. Using this device breathes specific energy into the new words and phrases more consciously. It is a technique often used to conceal proper names or secret messages. These cryptic messages can be simple or complex. They can be incorporated into poems and stories in much the same manner as a subliminal message. Anagrams also have been used as a form of divination (it involves using your own name), and they have even been used for such things as the sending of "love spells" through seemingly normal messages.

Anastrophe

An anastrophe is an inversion of the usual, logical order of the parts of a sentence. This is deliberately done to secure a rhythm more appropriate to the purpose of the poem or story, or for emphasis to make it register more strongly upon the psyche of an individual.

Assonance

This is a resemblance or similarity of sound between vowels with different consonants. This is not to be confused with rhyme which has a similarity between vowels and the same consonant. Knight and dike are words that fall under the category of assonance, while lake and fake would fall under the category of rhyme. Assonance is especially effective in maintaining the stimulation of a particular chakra center throughout the entire poem, but in a more subtle manner. With assonance, the similarity of sound does not always come at the end of a line. It is often intermingled within the lines themselves.

Chanson

This is a song composed of two-line stanzas of equal length, each followed by a refrain. The two-line poem or couplet is powerful in bringing together opposites into a new foundation. The two-line couplet with the two line refrain makes a four-line stanza. Four is the number of a new foundation.

Magical Quatrains

Magical quatrains, or poems with four lines, have been used by musico-magicians and poet-seers for ages. For magical purposes, the "quatrain" actually includes a fifth line. The first four lines use the same rhythm and the same pattern. they also describe the situation to be changed. The fifth line is an activation of the microcosmic forces within us all.

Five is the number of the microcosm, or humanity as a reflection of all the energies within the universe. The fifth line in the quatrain is the invoking of the Law of Correspondence—"As above, so below; as below, so above" —and the Law of Cause and Effect. It sets the energy into motion. The fifth line should employ your own name or the name of those for whom the forces are being invoked.

In Murry Hope's book *Practical Celtic Magic*, there is the story of someone named Corpry, who employed his bardic skills to compose a quatrain to undo his host Bres:[3]

> Without food quickly served,
> Without cow's milk, whereon a calf can grow,
> Without a dwelling fit for a man under the
>   gloomy night,
> Without means to entertain a bardic company,
> Let such be the condition of Bres!

This is just one example of the magical quatrain. With practice, you can develop your own quatrains, to be used as wonderful magical tools.

Meter and Rhythm

The kind of meter and rhythm used affects to a great degree the kind of rhythmic resonance experienced by the audience. Both aspects are found within the length of the stanza, the length of the line, and the length of the poem. All life has rhythm, and through the science of numerology, we can learn much of the esoteric significance of the rhythms employed in magical poetry.

The "Table of Rhythmic Correspondences" will provide a starting point for working with rhythmic correspondences in magical poetry. The numbers in the rhythm column can be applied to the number of beats in a line of poetry, the number of lines in a stanza, the number of repetitions of a word or phrase, or the numbers of patterns within the poetry. The poet magician must learn to construct the shape, form, and content of the poem with full intention and consciousness. In this way, even the meter adds to the magic of the poem, the incantation, or the prayer.

Meter is most often defined as a recurrence of a rhythmic pattern. This pattern in your magical poetry can facilitate the creation of resonance. (Keep in mind that many magical formulas include a rhythm of three, but even this depends upon the individual's purpose.)

Rhyme

Rhyme is the similarity and identity of sound. It is powerfully effective in establishing rhythm and form. It can be used to trigger stronger chakra resonance. Rhyme is found at the end of a line and at the beginning (within the first syllable), and it is also found internally as well.

Most people associate the rhyme with the end of a line. This is probably the easiest to construct and use, but it is not always the most effective. Forcing an end rhyme through improper rhythm and a sentence structure that is

TABLE OF RHYTHMIC CORRESPONDENCES

Rhythms	Energies, Effects, and Lessons of Rhythms
1	Aligns one to archetypal male energies; initiator; strength of will; discrimination; inventiveness; self-centeredness; laziness; fearfulness or fearlessness; lessons and energies of confidence; search for answers; independence and originality.
2	Aligns to rhythms of astral plane, archetypal feminine energy and dream consciousness; co-operative; kindness; psychic sensitivity; hypersensitivity; can be scattering; need to focus on details; vacillating and lessons of divisiveness; passion.
3	Aligns one to rhythms of saints and blessed souls; energies of art/inspiration; creativity; lessons of wastefulness and repression; spirituality and the awakening of the inner child; expressiveness (good or bad); optimism.
4	Aligns one to the rhythms of the Devas and Divine Men; energies of harmony/balance; building with patience; restricting and insensitive; narrow-mindedness; impracticality; solidarity; integration of energies/learnings from four corners of earth.
5	Aligns one to rhythms of Mother Nature herself; awakening of the microcosm of soul; lessons of freedom and purity; versatility; scattered, resists change and imposes rules; healing; adventuresome; freeing from limitations; psychic powers.

Table of Rhythmic Correspondences (Continued)

Rhythms	Energies, Effects, and Lessons of Rhythms
6	Aligns one with the feminine/mothering energies of the universe; nurturing energies; healing; birth-giving energy rhythms on all levels; rhythms of the educator; cynical and worrisome lessons; responsibility and reliability.
7	Aligns one to energies of all people and all planes; rhythms of healing for all systems; lessons of self-awareness and truth; rhythms of strong intuition; lessons of criticalness, melancholy and inferiority; wisdom and knowledge.
8	Aligns one to the energies of the gods and goddesses as they worked through nature in the past; unites physical rhythms of individual with spiritual ones; confidence; occult power; lessons of carelessness and authority; awakens true judgment of character.
9	Aligns one to ALL healing energies and experiences; rhythm of empathy and transitional forces in the universe; lessons of being hurt and overly sensitive; pessimism and indifference; intuitive love; rhythms of at-one-ment.

awkward will hinder any magical effects the rhyme could have accomplished.

Different rhymes serve different purposes. A rhyme at the beginning of the line is subtle, but it is a very effective way to trigger a chakra appropriate to the purpose of the poem. An internal rhyme is sometimes called the leonine rhyme. It has the capacity to touch the core of an individual's personality, triggering resonance below the surface ego.

Rhyme is also classified into the masculine and the feminine, which can be tied to the purpose and function of the magical poetry. A masculine rhyme is one that has a more forceful and more vigorous effect. The final, accented syllables are rhymed in a masculine rhyme. A feminine rhyme has a lightness and delicacy in movement that creates that same resonance in those that hear it. Feminine rhymes consist of the rhyming of two consecutive syllables. One syllable is stressed and the other is unstressed. It awakens lightness and grace. An example of a feminine rhyme would be "waken" and "forsaken." Also, long vowel sounds are generally considered more masculine, while the short vowel sounds are more feminine.

There are weak and there are strong rhymes that can be employed in magical poetry. If we are constructing poetry to help break old binding habits, using a weak rhyme in describing the old is effective, while using a strong rhyme to reflect the new energy you are creating is best. A weak rhyme is one in which the words are spelled differently but pronounced the same (e.g. rite and right). When accented syllables are rhymed, such as in "mating" and "waiting," then the rhyme is considered strong. When the unaccented syllables are rhymed, the rhyming is weak—such as in "forming" and "rating."

There is also a royal rhyme. This is a poem that has a magical rhythm of seven lines and it has a rhyme scheme of a-b-a-b-b-c-c. This royal rhyme has three rhymes within a seven-line poem. It is a form that has tremendous potential for magical and healing purposes.

Sonnet Magic

The sonnet is a powerful tool for magical poetry. It is a form that is beneficial to invoking creative and fertile energies into the consciousness. It has fourteen lines. The fourteenth path on the Qabalistic Tree of Life is the path of linking the primal male with the primal female forces of the universe. Whenever the male and female come together, birth occurs on some level. Both of the more common forms of the sonnet are comprised of fourteen lines.

The Italian or Petrarchan sonnet is traditionally two stanzas, one of eight lines and the last of six. In the first octave, the problem or question is expounded upon, and in the sextet the ideal resolution is described. The rhyme scheme for it is often a-b-b-a-a-b-b-a and c-d-e-c-d-e.

The Shakespearean or English sonnet has four divisions. There are three quatrains, each with their own rhyme scheme and a rhymed couplet which serves as the epigram. It calls for greater skill, but it is a powerful magical tool for constructing prayers and ritual invocations. The rhyme scheme follows a pattern similar to a-b-a-b/c-d-c-d/e-f-e-f/g-g.

CREATION OF THE PRAYER-POEM

Most words of power were not spoken, but rather they were intoned at length. They were extensions of the vocal tone. Each deity name was a prayer, a poem and a song to that deity. Many ritual prayers were designed to be sung or chanted. The magical poem serves as a means to open up once again to greater knowledge of the mystical forces of our lives.

The prayer-poems can be constructed to request assistance, to create opportunities, to heal, to awaken greater understanding, or to open to greater guidance.

There are no limits to its applications. The more the individual learns to consciously construct it and imbue it with greater significance, the more the poem can become an agent of change.

Poetry and prayer are most effective when used out-loud. Speaking it out loud sets into motion the energy of the magical construction. Much of the music and hymns were originally poems. The psalms are poetic hymns. Brahms "Lullaby" is comforting in both words and music.

Learning to create prayer-poems is a life task. It is not something to be dabbled in, for it works intimately with those forces operative behind all aspects of the Word. Learning to employ prayer-poems effectively awakens your own creative forces into a higher, more dynamic expression of life. As you learn to light your words with force and magic, your entire essence is touched by those same fires. And that is when the adventure and joy of life begins to unfold.

NOTES TO CHAPTER SEVEN

1. Johan Huizinga, *The Waning of the Middle Ages*, (London: Edward Arnold and Co., 1924) pp. 222–223 and 252–296. J. Huizinga also refers to the poet-seers in his article "Homo Ludens: A Study of the Play Element in Culture."

2. R. J. Stewart, *Underworld Initiation* (Northamptonshire: Aquarian Press, 1985) p. 171.

3. Murray Hope, *Practical Celtic Magic* (Northhamptonshire: Aquarian Press, 1987) p. 238.

CHAPTER EIGHT

Techniques of Bardic Healing

Anyone can be a bardic healer. The potential resides within us all. It does require a new look at ourselves and our world, and it demands a new sense of responsibility. The bardic tradition is about new perceptions. It is about responsibility for our lives and all those lives we touch. It is reminding ourselves that the finger pointing at the sun is not the same as the sun. It is within our own hearts that we hold all of our heavens and our hells—all that we can imagine and behold.

The ancient bards were the priest/ess magicians of their lives. They were healers at every moment. They were aware of every aspect of their being. Through their myths, tales, songs, and words they teach us what we can do.

In the Greek myths, Orpheus touched the heart of Eurydice with his songs and music, and their union was blessed. Tragedy struck: Eurydice was bitten by a snake and died. Orpheus played his song of grief and even the gods cried. Determined not to be forsaken, he took his song to the Underworld. Hades wept and all of the spirits of the dead were brought to a standstill. For the first time, even the Furies were wet with tears of sadness.

Moved by the song, Hades promised to return the beloved Eurydice to the upper world, as long as Orpheus would not look back until both had reached it. Anxious to see his beloved, he turned to look before she had exited the underworld passage. Eurydice was swept back down and lost forever to him.

Within this tale is much regarding the healing responsibilities we all face. All is possible within our lives as long as we learn to work with the laws and principles that govern our world. If not followed, a price will be paid. Our rewards and fulfillment will be incomplete.

The bardic tradition teaches us that we have a responsibility to all aspects of ourselves. There are certain natural laws that govern all life. We can only abuse the physical body so much before healing will not correct it. We need proper diet, exercise, rest, breathing and playtime to sustain the physical vehicle. Abuse of any of these will create imbalance. And even when things seem beyond our control—as in the case of Eurydice—the proper use of love, and knowledge of the healing arts can give us a second chance.

All aspects of the healing field, traditional and non-traditional, serve their purpose. It is not the intent of this work to give one method credence over another. The purpose is to show that there are always alternatives. There are many ways of healing and working with the human essence to restore balance. We each have our own unique energy system, and thus it is our responsibility to find that method or combination of methods that works best for us as individuals.

The techniques that follow are not meant to be a panacea for every health difficulty. Neither should they be taken as prescriptions. The techniques outlined are guidelines. We each must take those guidelines and reshape them and re-synthesize them into a method that works for us as individuals.

TUNING THE HUMAN ESSENCE

Tuning energies with voice, sound, or music will affect people in different ways, but since sound is basic to all life, it will affect everyone to varying degrees. Keep in mind that you are not practicing medicine. You are simply working with energy at primary levels. Regardless of the individual, there will be one common effect: sound treatments induce a comfortable state of relaxation.

For any of the techniques that follow within this chapter, you can use specific instruments to generate the sounds: pitch pipes, your own voice (with the vowel sounds), tuning forks, or any combination. I will describe the process using tuning forks, but as they can be expensive, you must simply adapt the process to your voice (or whatever methods you choose to use).

Regardless of what you use, it helps to visualize the vibration reaching out and restoring balance. There is an axiom of energy which states: "All energy follows thought." By visualizing the vibrations touching the chakra, restoring balance, and cleansing the individual of negative energy, the effects are amplified. Sound is effective. Thoughts are effective. Sound and thought together are extremely effective.

The individual can be seated or lying down during the tuning. It often depends on what you may intuit about the situation and the individual. The more comfortable the individual is, the more effective the tuning will be. I recommend working from the back, as the spine is a dynamic sound resonator, but there are times when working from the front is equally effective. It is also powerfully effective to place your hands on each of the points that you tone. This is especially effective in the "Humming Technique" described later in the chapter.

1. Have the individual assume an appropriate position —sitting or lying down.

2. Remind the individual to just relax and enjoy the session.

3. Cleanse and balance the auric field first. It can be done through the age-old technique of etheric or therapeutic touch to smooth out the ruffles in the aura. Simply hold your hands 6-8 inches from the body, and slowly stroke the energy surrounding the body. Visualize the electro-magnetic field of the individual smoothing itself out. It is very effective, if only in establishing a proper frame of mind for you and the other individual.

   Another method is to use incense, one that is calming and soothing. Smudging is an ancient process of cleansing and balancing an energy field. Having a calming scent in your healing area when the individual arrives will allow it to trigger resonance from that moment on.

   Tibetan cymbals are effective for straightening out the auric field. Or use soothing, recorded music to assist with this. The rattle, as previously discussed, is also effective for this.

4. Tune each chakra point along the spine. Use musical notes, vowel sounds, or tuning forks in any combination. Move through all seven chakra points.

5. After completing the first round, it is a good idea to cleanse the aura again. Balancing the chakras often releases negative static energy that has accumulated. Unless it is swept away, it may settle back in again.

6. Return to the tuning process, but use the entire chromatic scale. Use the sharps and flats, focusing on the in-between points along the spine. This opens and balances the meridians throughout the body.

7. Cleanse the aura again, to sweep out what may have been stirred up through this second phase of tuning.

8. Re-tune all seven chakras again. Sometimes the flow of energy that is re-established by opening and balancing the meridians can catch the chakras off guard and create another imbalance. This further ensures the strength and balance of the chakra energy.

9. Use any other healing techniques to cleanse the entire energy field of what has been released. A good smudging is effective. Various forms of channeled energy (etheric and therapeutic touch, spiritual laying on of hands, etc.) can be effective at this point. Use of a crystal or Tibetan singing bowl is a good method of shattering any energy debris and cleansing the aura.

10. "And that brings us back to DO. . ." Bring the session to an end. It is not unusual to have an individual fall asleep during the session. This is a good indication of the effectiveness. With any session, there should be discussion before and after. Counseling is an intricate part of the healing process. Ailments inform us of imbalances. They help us to discover negative patterns we have been creating on other levels. If we do not learn the lessons, the healing is temporary. It is a band-aid approach to health, and not holistic. If we can recognize the patterns, we can begin to change them. We do not want to merely treat symptoms, but causes as well.

TUNING THE HUMAN BODY

When working with the tuning forks to "tune" the body, one can work either from the front or the back. The tuning forks are being used to balance the chakra energy flow into the physical vehicle itself. Having the individual lie face down allows for work to be done along the spine. As previously discussed, the spine is an extremely strong sound resonator, and distributes the tones to the organs. It is not necessary to work along the spine; each must find what is suitable for him or her.

The tuning forks do not have to touch the body itself to have an effect. Simply holding them in the area of the chakra and close to the body is effective, although touching them to the spine also has its effects. (Some individuals feel that more healing occurs if the forks touch the spine. This is more psychological than actual, but whatever helps the client feel more at ease with the treatment will serve you both better.)

STEP ONE:

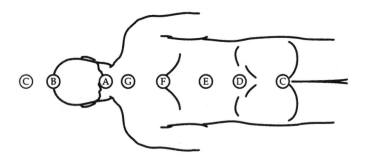

A. After positioning the person, strike each tuning fork for its own particular chakra.

B. Hold the tuning fork in the area of the chakra—just how long you hold it there depends upon you. Trust your intuition. Some you may feel the need to hold longer than others, and you may even feel the need to strike one a second time before moving on.

C. Start at the base chakra and move upward through ALL. Do not skip any chakras.

STEP TWO:

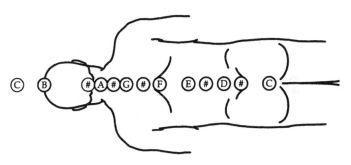

A. Step one serves the purpose of balancing the energy flow into the body and starts aligning the subtle bodies with the physical at the same time. Any static energy that may have accumulated in the chakras are virtually shaken loose by the intense vibration of the tuning forks.

B. We repeat the process, but this time use the entire chromatic scale with the tuning forks. For those tuning forks with a sharp or flat we strike and hold them along the area of the spine in between the tones and chakra points on either side. In other words, for the C# tone, we would strike it and hold it in the area between the base and spleen chakras, as depicted.

C. The thirteen tones of the chromatic scale not only balance the chakras, they also unblock and balance the energy pathways (meridians) from the chakras. Thus ALL of the energy flow is restored.

STEP THREE:

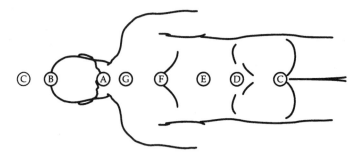

A. Unblocking and rebalancing the energy in steps one and two can send energy coursing into areas where it may not have been for a while. This can create a slight imbalance in the chakra which has not gotten use to the restored flow of energy. *This is why repeating step one is very important. It insures that the chakras are still balanced, even with the open and balanced meridians.*

B. Repeating step one also serves to give the chakras a little extra boost. If chakras have not been operating properly for a long while, they may try to slip back into the old pattern of distributing energy in an imbalanced manner. This step gives it extra strength and stability.

STEP FOUR:

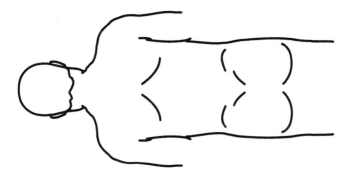

A. This step will vary from individual to individual. Some may want to channel energy into the person through etheric or therapeutic touch, or through some other form of spiritual healing.

B. It is at step four that I use the Tibetan singing bowl. The tuning forks would have released negative energy into the aura, energy that had become lodged. The bowl will shatter that energy, break up its pattern within the etheric body and restore the proper circulation of energy around the physical body.

C. The bowl can be played and moved up and down the spine. It can be set on the spine in the area that was causing the most difficulty.

Both methods are effective. It is interesting to note that if one listens closely while moving the bowl up and down the spine, subtle differences in the tone and vibration occur in its "singing" at the points of the chakras.

D. Some may wish to wait to channel healing energy (through spiritual methods or through etheric or therapeutic touch methods) until after the playing of the bowl. The bowl enhances the flow of energy into the individual and relieves the stress that may have been the initial cause of the difficulties.

This in no way implies that possession of the Tibetan bowl is an absolute necessity.

STEP FIVE:

A.   This is another opportunity to channel energy into the individual (aside from working with the sound). There are many techniques and books that demonstrate various ways of doing this.

B.   The Tibetan cymbals serve as excellent endings (and beginnings) for the session. They serve to set up a calming influence in the individual in the beginning and creates a new, fresh vibration for her/him to experience at the end of the session as he/she "awakens" from the altered state of consciousness that the sounds and tones instill through the balancing.

SPECIAL NOTES:

It is important to keep the proper state of mind throughout the entire process. Visualizing the energies of the individual balancing and flowing with health as you do each tone in each step enhances the procedures and its results. *Remember: All energy follows thought! Where you put your thoughts, that is where and how the energy will flow.*

Sometimes it is good to do an aura cleansing between each step. This is where the Tibetan cymbals are very effective. Striking them and running them down the body several times between each step serves to keep the negative, static energy that has been released from settling back into the chakras and physical body.

TUNING THE HUMAN BODY II

The method previously outlined can also be done in a seated position. It also does not necessarily entail the use of tuning forks and Tibetan bowls and cymbals. Any instrument can be used, but some do lend themselves more to this process. The voice also can be used.

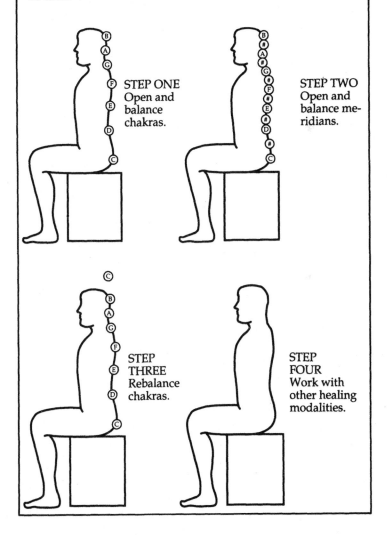

STEP ONE
Open and balance chakras.

STEP TWO
Open and balance meridians.

STEP THREE
Rebalance chakras.

STEP FOUR
Work with other healing modalities.

These are only guidelines. Each person must adapt them to his/her own needs and to the needs of the individuals he/she will be working with. There is no right or wrong. *Be advised that these methods are not intended to constitute medical advice or treatment.* They are simply methods of learning to work with our energies on all levels.

THY ROD AND THY STAFF

In a diatonic scale, there are seven primary notes—no sharps or flats. This would translate as C-D-E-F-G-A-B. As we have shown, these are keyed to the vibratory pattern of the seven major chakras. In our western octave, however, we do use sharps, flats, and half-tone intervals. Together they comprise thirteen tones, a very powerful and symbolic number in the science of numerology.

When we use all of the tones—including the sharps and flats—we not only balance out the chakras but the major energy pathways (meridians) as well. When used, the chromatic scale restores balance to the energy pathways. If there is congestion within a pathway, the tones will unblock them. If over-energized, the tones will restore them to their normal parameters.

Two of these meridians are critical to the overall functioning of the entire chakra system. One runs up the spine and is called the governing meridian. The other runs up the front median of the body and is called the conception meridian. They are sometimes referred to as the rod and staff. When the tones of middle C and high C are played, sung or toned, these two meridians are brought into balance. A microcosmic circuit of energy is established, linking the two.

The Psalms are a collection of religious songs, each serving a different purpose. These purposes range from

"THY ROD AND THY STAFF SHALL COMFORT ME"

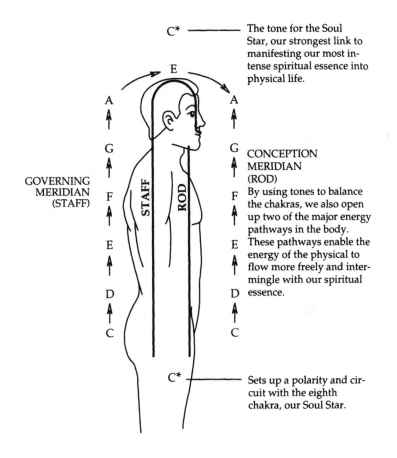

C* —————— The tone for the Soul Star, our strongest link to manifesting our most intense spiritual essence into physical life.

CONCEPTION MERIDIAN (ROD)
By using tones to balance the chakras, we also open up two of the major energy pathways in the body. These pathways enable the energy of the physical to flow more freely and intermingle with our spiritual essence.

C* —————— Sets up a polarity and circuit with the eighth chakra, our Soul Star.

GOVERNING MERIDIAN (STAFF)

*The tones of Middle C and High C enable the circuit of energy between the meridians to be connected, thus allowing a freer and more balanced flow of energy.

healing, to restoring joy, to celebrating life, to passing on esoteric teachings. Some were composed for liturgical use in the temples. In many current Bibles, there is information concerning the word origins, the tone in which they were to be played, and even the instrument to be used.

The Twenty-third Psalm—the most commonly recognized of all—has great esoteric significance. The rod and the staff mentioned within it are ancient symbols of spiritual strength, balance and protection when opening to greater spiritual heights. As you can see in the diagram on the previous page, the tones that balance the major chakras and meridians actually take on the formation of a shepherd's staff and rod. Add this to the fact that most of the Psalms were musical songs, it can then be rightly inferred that music was well-understood and used by the ancient Hebrew seers.

Singing, toning, or humming the chromatic scale will activate and balance these two meridians. It is important to place the tongue against the upper front teeth while doing so, as this connects the two meridians. As you inhale, draw the energy up the spine, and then as you exhale, let it flow down the front of the body. Use one inhalation for each tone, toning it silently as you inhale and then toning it audibly as you exhale.

Repeat this with each tone of the chromatic scale: C-C#-D-D#-E-F-F#-G-G#-A-A#-B-C. This balances all of the chakras and the major meridians of the body. It strengthens the auric field, and it can be used to generate energy to hasten the healing process. When these centers and meridians are balanced in this manner, the "rod and staff" truly comfort. This can be done by yourself, or it can be done to another individual. If working on another person, coordinate your toning with their breathing rhythms.

THE HEALING HUM

We often hear the phrase "whistle while you work," but more appropriate would be "humming while you work." The humming sound is a powerful tool. It carries sounds internally. It establishes rapport between our spiritual aspects and our emotional/mental and physical aspects. It brings them into harmony. In this lies the answer to much of the power of the mantra "Om." Humming actually performs a micro-massage upon the internal organs, releasing stress and restoring balance. It creates sympathy, harmony, and poise.

We have seen how the vowels will open particular parts of the human body, especially in the toning process. Adding the humming sound at the end of a vowel toning, carries the sound more deeply into the body. For example, instead of just toning the long E sound as "eeee," add an "M." It then becomes "eeemmm." This is particularly helpful when toning for yourself, as you will be able to feel the internal vibration much more easily.

When working on another individual, place your hands on the appropriate spot on the spine as you hum the tone. This will enhance the effects upon this individual. The humming vibration is carried through your body, vibrating down your arms and out your hands to more forcefully impact with his/her energies.

SINGING

Singing is one of our most creative acts. It links us to our underlying substance and being. It is a means by which we can enter into a relationship with our most occult powers and abilities. Words in and of themselves have power, but when those words are sung, that power becomes universal.

Singing involves full use of the voice and our self. We are an instrument of sound and music. Singing helps us to breathe more fully. It can improve the posture, enhance our speaking voice, and helps bring emotional awareness and fulfillment. It helps when we are toning for health. It serves as a grounding mechanism, as well as one to attain greater spiritual heights. One who sings, prays twice.

Music and singing awaken our own creativity. Listening to it will stimulate movement and thought. Singing releases stress. It enables us to participate in learning skills and disciplines that reflect higher principles.

There are many ways of using your voice in a more joyful manner to enhance your health. Singing expresses who we are. We are creating sound where there was silence. We produce sound in the same way that the divine produced the world. Most of us have lost the joy of this creative process. Singing restores the ability to create. By re-learning how to play with our voices, we find we can affect everything about us—animate or inanimate.

1. Pick a melody that you enjoyed singing as a child.

2. Sing it, varying the volume in different parts of the song.

3. Make pauses within the song for dramatic effect.

4. Sing the song with a foreign accent.

5. Sing the song with nonsense words instead of the normal lyrics.

6. Pretend you are singing the song to a lover or special friend.

7. Try to sing the melody like various professionals.

8. Sing the song as if extremely bashful.

9. Sing the song with confidence.

10. Sing the song with the same vowel sound in every syllable.

Learn to play with your voice and with your singing. We all enjoyed singing at one time, and we can recapture that joy and our balance in the process. What normally happens with these processes is that it creates laughter, and laughter is healing. These exercises release tension and stress, and facilitate the process of toning.

Our songs can moderate our passions and shatter energy around us to any degree we desire. Singing is a way of cleansing the etheric body, so as to strengthen the flow of energy into the physical. It is like cleaning the filter of a faucet, so that the water runs full and clean into the glass we will be drinking from.

In the ancient bardic traditions, the students and the teachers sang so as to absorb their own sounds and vibrations. Once their thoughts and feelings were formulated, they needed to be grounded into the physical realm. Singing allowed this to occur. They knew the sounds were communicated to the throat by the energies of the soul itself, and by working with the sounds, they could bring more light from the soul into the physical realm. The light and darkness of the soul determined the quality of the voice. By working with sound and singing for its healing properties, they could overcome any darkness within the soul. The voice would then in turn take on greater resonance and quality.

The ancient singers sang to the quality of their own voice. They worked to express themselves—not a tradition or an imitation of someone they found pleasing. They knew it was possible for humanity to escape the tensions and stresses of the physical world through singing. They could maintain their balance and thus not experience the detrimental effects of their environment or their associations.

They employed various methods. Some melodies they would simply sing. They would hum things to correct their moods, and they would employ chanting—singularly or in groups. The chant or plainsong was a particularly effective technique in that it activated the energies of the upper chakras. Through chants they produced greater communion with the divine spark that existed within themselves. The Gregorian chants that we know today are still powerful tools of consciousness. They inspire awe and wonder at the mystery of the divine. They are cleansing to any negative environment. (We have all experienced entering a room where we know a fight or argument has occurred. The tension is tangibly felt. Playing a Gregorian chant for ten minutes will shatter all of that tension and negative energy, so that nothing can be detected.)

Music and voice trains us in harmony, but we must learn to use the sacred song word again. "The song word is powerful; it names a thing, it stands at the sacred center, drawing all towards it. . . The word disappears, the poetry is gone, but the imagined form persists within the mind and works upon the soul!"[1]

GROUP HEALING WITH SACRED SOUND

The schools of wisdom had specific healing rooms and temples. Sound and music were a part of their lives. The singing took the form of chanting, mantras, poetry—as well as the form we now call song. The toning process was used in healing in conjunction with a person's astrological chart. Groups of healers would tone or sing a variation of sounds associated with the astrological aspect, while surrounding the individual in specific geometric configurations.

Geometric shapes alter and focus electro-magnetic energies. They can serve to amplify or direct sound energy more specifically for an individual's healing problem. The healers could also align themselves in a configuration of the astrological chart and emit a series of tones to restore the person's energy field to its most natural state—the state in which it entered into incarnation.

Geometrical shapes set up a tuning through chords—a combination of tones. For example, a pyramid or triangular configuration can be utilized to amplify energy tremendously. The individual angles do affect the energy, but for the beginner, it is best to use an equilateral form. Three healers are needed, each taking a position an equal distance apart from each other and the person to be healed.

An entire sequence of tones can be directed by the three. Or astrological aspects can be employed in deciding which tones to use. Earlier we discussed the tones associated with the Sun sign, Moon sign and Ascendant in the astrological chart. The three healers can use the tones for these and project them at the individual in the middle of their triangle. The healers can use the "Om" or they may wish to use the primary vowel sound in the first name of

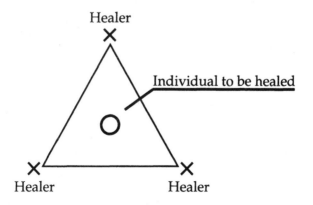

Healing is enhanced by geometrical formations.

the individual to be healed. In essence, this sets up a chord which triggers a tremendous amount of energy and overtones. These are amplified by the geometrical shape in which they are being projected.

Meditation and healing groups can have tremendous fun and wonderful effects by using these processes. It is a wonderful way to feel and prove the effects for oneself. Each individual of the group can take turns in the middle of the group, while they tone sounds and notes in various geometric shapes. It also creates group harmony, so group toning is an effective process to do prior to any ritual or ceremonial work.

The use of geometric shapes around an individual while toning is very powerful. In the East, the use of geometric shapes is called yantra and geomancy. Yantras are essentially visual tools to help in centering. When used for healing or worship purposes, the energy associated with them is invoked and symbolizes some divine aspect of the universe. When used in conjunction with toning, that divine aspect becomes grounded into the physical to impact and stimulate healing energies. When the group forms about an individual in a yantric or geometric shape, they create a vortex of energy within that shape. As they tone, that energy is set in motion.

Groups and circles are highly effective for projecting long-distance healing tones to individuals. Depending upon the particular problem, the group decides on a geometric form and the tones to be used. Then they visualize the individual needing the healing, picturing he/she in the center of the circle. As they tone, they visualize the energy going forth to touch the individual. Placing a picture in the middle is also effective, as it assists the group in their visualization, and the picture is a direct link to that individual.

A study of the symbolism of geometric shapes will reveal much wisdom regarding how to use them in group toning and healing. The following are examples (and they by no means cover the spectrum) of energies associated with the various shapes. Many of the geometric shapes may have to be adapted to the number of healing circle members. These are guidelines. The more you learn about the power and energy created by geometric shapes, the more energy you can project when the toning is applied.

SQUARE
Forming a square about an individual while toning provides greater stability and equilibrium to the individual. It calms and settles. It also amplifies the life force energy of the base chakra. It is very grounding to an individual's energies.

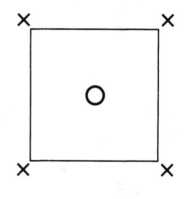

TRIANGLE
The triangle has already been alluded to. It strongly affects the spleen chakra and it can be used to heat up or cool down the system. It enables the tones to have an amplified cleansing effect.

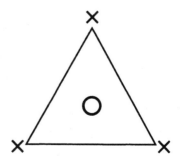

CIRCLE

The circle is the most natural and perfect shape in nature. It builds an energy vortex of totality and wholeness when used with toning. It enhances the sounds so that they create new life and energy within the individual. The circle is the womb. it sets up a force that links the divine with the human, the inner with the outer. It can be used with problems associated with the solar plexus chakra, and it can be used when no other shape seems appropriate.

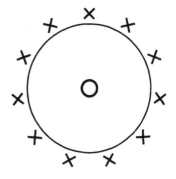

THE CROSS

The cross sets up an energy that balances the four elements of the body. It strongly affects the heart chakra and all problems associated with it. When used with toning, it links and balances the four energies of humanity—physical, emotional, mental, and spiritual. The tones with the cross create a balance of polarities—the balanced male and female.

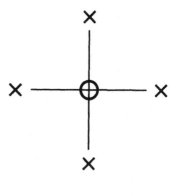

THE CRESCENT

The crescent is a shape that will enhance healing of emotions and problems of expression when used with toning. It is linked to the throat chakra. It can be used to bring out the feminine energies of illumination, imagination, and intuition. It is a tremendous amplifier of tonal effects.

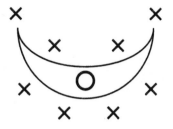

THE SIX-RAYED STAR (on the points of a circle)

This figure, when used with toning, links the heart and the mind, the lower and the higher, the divine and the human. It brings the divine into play within the physical dimension. It affects the brow and the heart chakras. It can be used with toning to set up an energy that is strengthening and protecting. It helps to activate inner solar fires.

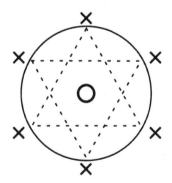

THE FIVE-POINTED STAR (on the points of a circle)

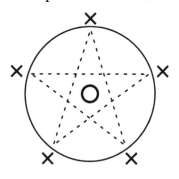

When used with toning, the five-pointed star is balancing and grounding. It activates the energies of the individual so that there is dominion of spirit over the four elements, reason over matter. It helps to provide a concentrated force of spirit. When used with sound and music, it draws angels of strength and energy, especially those known as the Seraphim.

THE SEVEN-RAYED STAR (on the points of a circle)

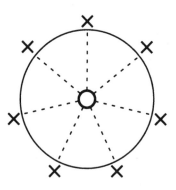

This shape, when used with toning, is extremely healing on all levels. Seven is the mystical number, and this figure assists in balancing all of the chakras, subtle bodies, and physiological systems of humanity. It creates a vortex that invokes the play of energies from the seven major planets of the ancients and the seven rays of light. It is soothing to the emotions and is a powerful amplifier of healing energies for children. This shape is often called the star of St. Bridgette, protector and healer of children.

CONCENTRIC CIRCLES

This particular configuration of three concentric circles of healers surrounding the triangle is more than a healing mandala for sound. It is a confirmation that can be used with groups to do explorations of time—past, present, and future. When used with meditation upon the one being healed, it can reveal the karma of the illness. It can also be used to determine if present actions will result in future illnesses. Its many uses have yet to be fully explored.

With each of the individual configurations, the one to be healed sits within the center. They are the point of receptivity for the healing sounds. In tantra, the point is called the bindu, which represents the supreme consciousness. In healing, it is this consciousness which needs to be affected in order to instill the balancing.

Part of the spiritual quest for any individual is to find the spiritual center within—the center which has all power and all balance and all healing. By placing the individual in the center, the healers are symbolically setting up a link to his or her interior, spiritual center. The individual is also protected by the circle of healers. They keep negative energy out so that the positive can do its utmost work.

The center is the nucleus of the circle. It is the focus of love and the focus of the healing energies of sound being poured out by the other members onto the individual. It is only by being in the center that we can establish a relationship with the divine. In this case, it is the healing aspect of the divine.

HEALING WITH SOUND AND CRYSTALS

Science and metaphysics are both proving that there are many ways in which gems, stones, and crystals affect the wearer. When stress is applied to a crystalline stone, it elicits a form of electrical energy, known as piezoelectrical energy. This stress can be the simple pressure of someone holding it within the hand or the pressure of wave pulsations that occur with sound and music.

The sound waves trigger a release of energy from the stone according to its own unique structure. For this reason, certain stones and certain tones are very compatble. The energy of both have a comparable pattern that when used together, they reinforce each other. As seen on the chart on the next page, certain stones and tones will affect the same areas of the body.

The history of utilizing stones and sound in the healing process is ancient. Sound frequencies were used for healing and for heightened consciousness. Gemstones were arranged in acoustical patterns. The mystery traditions of India, Egypt, Babylon, and Greece employed both tools.

There are many ways in which sound and crystals can be used for healing and the raising of consciousness. They work whether a person realizes it or not. They do so because they are miniature dynamos of energy (of varying frequencies). There are those who say they do not feel the energy, but when crystals are used with sound, the effects are heightened and more tangible. The combination restores balance and releases stress, sometimes shattering the negative patterns that have accumulated in the individual's energy field.

HEALING WITH SOUND AND STONE

(With all of the chakras and tones, clear quartz can be used to amplify or to supplement when specific stones can not be found.)

Chakra	Tone	Crystal and Stones	Effects of Stones and Sounds
Base	C	Smoky Quartz (and all red stones)	Purifies base chakra; channels energy from crown into the base; very grounding; helps dissolve negativity; affects all physical aspects of this chakra.
Spleen	D	Carnelian, Citrine (and all orange stones)	Affects adrenals and all physical aspects of chakra; stimulates creativity; assists in visualizations & manifestation; can be used to release past life information.
Solar	E	Citrine, Topaz (and all yellow stones)	Stimulates cosmic awareness; balances left brain; can be used with visualization to attract; can help link the mental with the intuitive aspects of self.
Heart	F	Rose Quartz, Amethyst, Tourmaline (and all green stones)	Healing and balancing; stimulates immune system; calming; helps heal internal wounds—past life wounds; awakens sense of fulfillment.
Throat	G	Turquoise, Tourmaline and all light blue stones	Stimulates creativity; opens up greater self-expression; will draw out negativity; affects breathing.
Brow	A	Lapus Lazuli, Sodalite, Flourite	Clear thinking; headaches; balances right & left hemispheres; opens clairvoyance; cleansing to aura; penetrating mental blocks.
Crown	B	Amethyst, Flourite, Clear Quartz	Purifying to the entire system; affects skeletal system strongly; awakens greater humility; balances aura.

The spine is an excellent transmitter of the energies of stone, just as it is with sound. The methods described earlier for working with the spine can be enhanced by laying specific crystals and stones along the various vertabrae.

We are all scientists in the making and we are all magicians. It does require effort and discipline and work, but such tasks and explorations are to be savored and enjoyed. It is not the end that brings the rewards, but it is the path that we take to that end that holds the real treasures!

AFTERTHOUGHTS

Know thyself. This was the precept of the ancient mystery schools, and it must again become a precept of our own lives. We do not have to give up our responsibilities. We can learn to use energies and abilities long forgotten but still available. Within each of us are all of the energies and forces of the universe. Within each of us is the potential to manifest greater fulfillment, abundance, health and awareness into all arenas of our lives.

The bards worked through their stories and songs to keep alive the magic and wonder of life. They reminded people that every tree, bush and rock spoke. They helped people to hear the whispers of the wind and the songs of the animals. They awakened the child within all who would listen. They kept the seeds of creative joy alive.

The Seed

The small child looked out over the yard from the roof of his house. He backed up a few steps and took a deep breath. With a running start and a squeal of laughter, he leaped from the roof into the air. And he was flying.

"Son," cried his father, coming out of the house. "Come down here this instant! Little boys are not meant to fly!"

The boy looked down at his angry father, puzzled by his reaction.

"Why not?" asked the child. And he promptly flew away.

"Of all the disrespect!" muttered his father, and he stormed back into his house.

NOTES TO CHAPTER EIGHT

1. J. Halifax, *Shamanic Voices* (New York: Dutton, 1979), p. 33.

SELECT BIBLIOGRAPHY

1. SOUND, MUSIC AND VOICE

Clynes, Manfred. *Music, Mind and Brain.* New York: Plenum Press, 1983.

Crandall, Joanne. *Self-Transformation Through Music.* Wheaton: Theosophical Publishing, 1986.

Da Silva, Andrew J. *Do From the Octave of Man Number Four.* New York: Borderline Press, 1985.

David, William. *The Harmonics of Sound, Color and Vibration.* DeVorss: California, 1980.

Dickinson, Edward. *Music in the History of the Western Church.* New York: Charles Scribner's Sons, 1902.

Drury, Neville. *Music For Inner Space.* California: Prism Press, 1985.

Godwin, Joscelyn. *Harmonies of Heaven and Earth.* New York: Inner Traditions International, 1987.

Hall, Manly P. *The Therapeutic Value of Music Including the Philosophy of Music.* Los Angeles: Philosophical Research Society, 1982.

Hamel, Peter Michael. *Through Music to the Self.* New York: Dorset, 1978.

Heline, Corinne. *Beethoven's Nine Symphonies Correlated With the Nine Spiritual Mysteries.* Santa Monica: New Age Bible and Philosophy Center, 1986.

_____. *Music: The Keynote of Human Evolution*. Santa Monica: New Age Bible and Philosophy Center; 1986.

_____. *The Cosmic Harp*. Santa Monica: New Age Bible and Philosophy Center, 1986.

_____. *Star Gates*. Santa Monica: New Age Bible and Philosophy Center, 1986.

_____. *The Esoteric Music of Richard Wagner*. Santa Monica: New Age Bible and Philosophy Center, 1986.

Heline, Theodor. *The Archetypes Unveiled*. Los Angeles: New Age Press, 1986.

Jeans, Sir James. *Science and Music*. New York: Dover Publications, 1968.

Katsh, Shelley and Merle-Fishman, Carol. *The Music Within You*. New York: Simon and Schuster, Inc., 1985.

Halpern, Steven. *Tuning the Human Instrument*. California: Spectrum Research, 1978.

_____. *Sound Health*. California: Spectrum Research,

Keyes, Laurel. *Toning—the Creative Power of Voice*. California: DeVorss, 1973.

Langacker, Ronald W. *Language and its Structure*. New York: Harcourt, Brace and World, Inc., 1968.

Lewis, Robert C. *The Sacred Word and its Overtones*. Oceanside: Rosicrucian Fellowship, 1986.

Lingerman, Hal A. *The Healing Energies of Music*. Wheaton: Theosophical Publishing, 1983.

McClain, Ernest G. *The Pythagorean Plato*. York Beach, ME: Nicolas-Hayes, Inc., 1978.

_____. *The Myth of Invariance*. York Beach, ME: Nicolas-Hayes, Inc., 1976.

Nemmers, Erwin Esser. *Twenty Centuries of Catholic Church Music*. Milwaukee: Bruce Publishing Company, 1949.

Rudhyar, Dane. *The Rebirth of Hindu Music*. New York: Weiser, 1979.

Khan, Hazrat Inayat. *The Mysticism of Sound*. Geneva: International Headquarters of Sufi Movement, 1979.

Robertson, Stuart and Cassidy, Frederick G. *The Development of Modern English*. Englewood Ciffs, NJ: Prentice Hall, Inc., 1954.

Ross, Raymond S. *Speech Communication*. Englewood Cliffs, NJ: Prentice Hall Inc., 1970.

Steiner, Rudolph. *The Inner Nature of Music and the Experience of Tone*. New York: Anthroposophic Press, 1983.

Stewart, R.J. *Music and the Elemental Psyche*. New York: Destiny Books, 1987.

Tame, David. *The Secret Power of Music*. New York: Destiny Books, 1984.

Levarie, Siegmund and Levy, Ernst. Tone: *A Study in Musical Acoustics*. Westport, CT: Greenwood Press, 1981.

2. THE BARDIC TRADITIONS

Bauer, Caroline Feller. *Handbook for Storytellers*. Chicago: American Library Association, 1977.

Bettelheim, Bruno. *The Uses of Enchantment*. New York: Alfred A. Knopf, 1976.

Bogin, Meg. *The Women Troubadours*. New York: Paddington Press, 1976.

Breneman, Lucille. *Once Upon a Time*. Chicago: Nelson-Hall Pub., 1983.

Danielson, Francis Weld. *Practice Story Telling Class*. Chicago: Pilgrim Press, 1920.

Dundes, Alan. *The Study of Folklore*. Englewood Cliffs, NJ: Prentice-Hall, 1965.

Goldron, Romain. *Minstrels and Masters*. New York: H.S. Struttman, 1968.

Harrington, W.L. *Talking Well*. New York: Macmillan, 1924.

Hurley, Richard James. *Campfire Tonight*. Michigan: Peak Press, 1940.

Lowry, Shirley Park. *Familiar Mysteries: The Truth in Mythology*. New York: Oxford University Press, 1982.

Pellowski, Anne. *The World of Storytelling*. New York: Bowker Company, 1977.

Sawyer, Ruth. *The Way of the Storyteller*. New York: Viking Press, 1942.

Tatar, Maria. *The Hard Facts of Grimms' Fairy Tales*. Princeton, NJ: Princeton University Press, 1987.

Yolen, Jane, Ed. *Favorite Folktales From Around the World*. New York: Pantheon Books, 1986.

Index

☾ LLEWELLYN ORDERING INFORMATION

Order Online:
Visit our website at www.llewellyn.com, select your books, and order them on our secure server.

Order by Phone:
- Call toll-free within the U.S. at 1-877-NEW-WRLD (1-877-639-9753). Call toll-free within Canada at 1-866-NEW-WRLD (1-866-639-9753)
- We accept VISA, MasterCard, and American Express

Order by Mail:
Send the full price of your order (MN residents add 6.5% sales tax) in U.S. funds, plus postage & handling to:

Llewellyn Worldwide
2143 Wooddale Drive, Dept. 978-0-87542-018-9
Woodbury, MN 55125-2989

Postage & Handling:

Standard (U.S., Mexico, & Canada). If your order is:
   $24.99 and under, add $3.00
   $25.00 and over, FREE STANDARD SHIPPING

AK, HI, PR: $15.00 for one book plus $1.00 for each additional book.

International Orders (airmail only):
   $16.00 for one book plus $3.00 for each additional book

Orders are processed within 2 business days.
Please allow for normal shipping time. Postage and handling rates subject to change.

How to Meet & Work with Spirit Guides

TED ANDREWS

We often experience spirit contact in our lives but fail to recognize it for what it is. Now you can learn to access and attune to beings such as guardian angels, nature spirits and elementals, spirit totems, archangels, gods and goddesses—as well as family and friends after their physical death.

Contact with higher soul energies strengthens the will and enlightens the mind. Through a series of simple exercises, you can safely and gradually increase your awareness of spirits and your ability to identify them. You will learn to develop an intentional and directed contact with any number of spirit beings. Discover meditations to open up your subconscious. Learn which acupressure points effectively stimulate your intuitive faculties. Find out how to form a group for spirit work, use crystal balls, perform automatic writing, attune your aura for spirit contact, use sigils to contact the great archangels, and much more! Read *How to Meet and Work with Spirit Guides* and take your first steps through the corridors of life beyond the physical.

978-0-7387-0812-6
216 pp., illus.   **$9.95**

How To
Uncover Your Past Lives

Ted Andrews

How to Uncover Your Past Lives
TED ANDREWS

Knowledge of your past lives can be extremely reward-ing. It can assist you in opening to new depths within your own psychological makeup. It can provide greater insight into present circumstances with loved ones, career and health. It is also a lot of fun.

Now Ted Andrews shares with you nine different tech-niques that you can use to access your past lives. Between techniques, Andrews discusses issues such as karma and how it is expressed in your present life, the source of past life information, soul mates and twin souls, proving past lives, the mysteries of birth and death, animals and rein-carnation, abortion and premature death, and the role of reincarnation in Christianity.

To explore your past lives, you need only use one or more of the techniques offered. Complete instructions are provided for a safe and easy regression. Learn to dowse to pinpoint the years and places of your lives with great accuracy, make your own self-hypnosis tape, attune to the incoming child during pregnancy, use the tarot and the cabala in past life meditations, keep a past life journal, and more.

978-0-7387-0813-3
192 pp., illus.   **$8.95**